Praise for

Legion

"Shadia has written another outstanding study. *Legion* is rich and in-depth. There were so many new insights; several brought tears to my eyes. Well written and well organized, this study is packed with valuable life lessons. I can't wait to read the next one!"

—**Francine Rivers,** international best-selling author

"Shadia combines brilliant biblical insights with thought-provoking applications as she unfolds the stirring story of the man known as Legion. Though one of the more obscure individuals to experience Christ's powerful rescuing love, this man's life is destined to become a much-loved Bible story as Shadia leads you into his broken world. I highly recommend this stunning, thorough, unforgettable, hope-filled Bible study."

—**Dr. Phyllis Bennett,** director of the Women's Center for Ministry at Western Seminary

"When I opened the cover of *Legion*, I knew to expect something special. Shadia has proven again and again to be such a gifted, kind, patient, and wise Bible teacher. What I didn't expect was such a wide-ranging study of who God is, how much he loves us, and what good things he offers. Exploring one of the most overlooked and misunderstood miracles of Jesus, this powerful study offers a step-by-step approach to understanding God and his work in a deeper way. If you want to get to know God better, Shadia is a wonderful guide."

—**Susy Flory,** *New York Times* best-selling author and director of the West Coast Christian Writers Conference

"In this excellent, in-depth study, Shadia invites us on roads less-traveled to find the courage to face the deep struggles that often leave us feeling helpless and hopeless. Journeying through the biblical story of Legion while sharing parts of her own, Shadia comes alongside her readers with relevancy and compassion, revealing a holy, merciful God who desires to break through our toughest walls and rescue us. Powerful, personal, and life-changing!"

—**Jan Kern,** author, speaker, and cofounder of Voice of Courage

"We've all wrestled with the question of how God can be good when there's so much evil in the world. In *Legion*, Shadia explores that question and more in the retelling of an ancient Gospel story that graphically illustrates the depths of evil and God's gracious, compassionate response. Her in-depth research and attention to detail make this study well worth reading!"

—**Bruce W. Martin,** author of *Desperate for Hope*

Praise for

Tamar and Hagar

"From the first pages of this in-depth Bible study on Tamar, Shadia Hrichi reveals her knowledge of Scripture and her desire for us to be transformed by truth. With consideration for the whole counsel of God's Word, Hrichi dives deep into the story of an abandoned woman to show us that God makes the powerless secure and invites the abandoned to belong."

—**Shawna Marie Bryant,** podcaster and author of *Longing to Belong: Discovering the Joy of Acceptance*

"After going through Shadia's Bible study on Hagar, I couldn't wait to see what she would do next. *Tamar* is another outstanding Bible study, rich in historical detail, cultural insights, and applicable life lessons for us today. I appreciate Shadia sharing personal stories from her own life (some heartbreaking, some amusing), which help shine light on Tamar's story. Perfect for personal and/or group study."

—**Francine Rivers,** international best-selling author

"I have never felt so connected to an author while reading a Bible Study. Shadia Hrichi is a refreshingly real and relatable, grace-filled guide who roots this heartbreaking account within its historical context and God's plan of redemption. Witnessing Tamar's transformation from a mistreated, abandoned young widow into a powerful catalyst for change illuminates what God can accomplish through us and in us, even in the midst of our most painful circumstances. For anyone who has ever felt betrayed or deceived, this study is a blessing and a balm."

—**Rosie Makinney,** author, podcaster, and founder of Fight For Love Ministries

"Shadia is an engaging and knowledgeable guide who holds her reader's hand throughout the broader story of Tamar, while still creating room for individuals to listen for God's truth specifically for them. She integrates passages from both the Old and New Testaments, so those looking for an interactive but comprehensive approach to understanding the biblical narrative will be equipped to dive deep into this story of redemption."

—**Andrea Coli,** teaching pastor and Christian speaker

"Few biblical stories illustrate hope in the hard places of life better than Hagar's. Shadia Hrichi beautifully illuminates that hope, offering encouragement not only for the destination of our lives, but also for the journey. Through this study, readers will be inspired to trust God, embrace His purposes, and experience His victory."

—**Chris Tiegreen,** author of the *Dancing in the Desert Devotional Bible*

"A Bible study on Sarah's Egyptian slave girl? I've never done a study on Hagar before, but Shadia reveals that there is more to Hagar's story than meets the eye. Used and abandoned . . . where was God in that? I've also wrestled with this question at times. Who hasn't? Thank you, Shadia, for opening my eyes to Hagar's story; in doing so, it helped me to see myself."

—**Kay Marshall Strom,** author and international speaker

God Is Always Working

BEHIND THE SEEN

LEGION

Rediscovering the God Who Rescues Me

Shadia Hrichi

LEAFWOOD
PUBLISHERS
an imprint of Abilene Christian University Press

LEGION

Rediscovering the God Who Rescues Me

LEAFWOOD PUBLISHERS
an imprint of Abilene Christian University Press

ISBN 978-1-68426-370-7 | LCCN 2019016670

Printed in the United States of America

LIBRARY OF CONGRESS CATALOGING-IN-PUBLICATION DATA
Names: Hrichi, Shadia, 1967- author.
Title: Legion : rediscovering the God who rescues me / by Shadia Hrichi.
Description: Abilene, Texas : Leafwood Publishers, 2019. | Series: Behind
the seen: exploring the Bible's unsung heroes
Identifiers: LCCN 2019016670 | ISBN 9781684263707 (pbk.)
Subjects: LCSH: Healing of the Gerasene demoniac (Miracle)—Textbooks. |
Spiritual healing—Textbooks.
Classification: LCC BT367.H38 H75 2019 | DDC 232.9/55—dc23
LC record available at https://lccn.loc.gov/2019016670

Cover design by Thinkpen Design
Interior text design by Sandy Armstrong, Strong Design

Leafwood Publishers is an imprint of Abilene Christian University Press
ACU Box 29138
Abilene, Texas 79699

1-877-816-4455
www.leafwoodpublishers.com

26 27 28 29 30 / 7 6 5 4 3

CONTENTS

Acknowledgments 7

About the Author 9

About the Study 11

Group Study Tips 13

A Note from the Author 15

Part I: The Bondage

Week One: Reflecting on God's Risk 19

Week Two: Awaiting God's Reign 53

Part II: The Battle

Week Three: Seeking God's Refuge 87

Week Four: Experiencing God's Restoration 119

Week Five: Embracing God's Rescue 151

Part III: The Blessing

Week Six: Entering God's Rest 187

Leader Guide 220

Tips for a Sabbath Date with Jesus 221

ACKNOWLEDGMENTS

EACH ONE OF US IS CREATED BY GOD FOR A PURPOSE. However, in order for each of us to fulfill that purpose, we need each other. Scripture describes us as "one body" but "many parts." I confess that there is not enough room here to recognize every person whom God, in His grace, has brought alongside me in some way as this ministry grows. Nevertheless, I wish to personally thank those who were involved in the development or support of this study.

Thank you, Leafwood Publishers! From concept review to copyediting, cover and interior design, production, sales, and marketing, your commitment to excellence shines forth every step of the way. I am especially grateful to Jason Fikes for his exceptional insight and skill during the content review and to Rebecka Scott and Laura Homer for their superb editing. Thank you, also, to Duane Anderson and all the rest of the saints at Leafwood for all that you do for the kingdom. It is a true honor to partner with you!

To my dear friends Sandi Miller, Linda Dunning, Karen Mutsch, and Kendra Burrows who devoted countless hours serving as beta readers for this study: your excellent feedback and suggestions provided invaluable insights, and your gentle encouragement along the way helped me to persevere to the end. Thank you!

I also wish to express my deep gratitude to the leadership at Venture Christian Church, particularly Women's Minister Tricia Christensen, for all the ways you have supported me over the years. I am thankful to you, along with my entire church family (at Venture and beyond), for your love, prayers, gifts, and support. Truly, we are "one body" but "many parts."

To so many wonderful friends and family, including Carolyn Jacobsen, Liz Nunez, Sandi Miller, and so many others: thank you for the numerous ways you have supported me as God continues to expand this ministry. Your delicious meals,

ongoing prayers, ministry support, and logistical help, along with your enduring love and friendship, bless me more than you can know.

To Francine Rivers: truly, your friendship, support, and ongoing encouragement continue to be such a tremendous blessing to me. Thank you for your willingness to read and endorse this study!

To Phyllis Bennett, Bruce W. Martin, Susy Flory, and Jan Kern: I am deeply grateful to each of you for your friendship and support, and especially your sacrifice of time in reading and endorsing this work. Thank you!

To all the saints who have served at the Mount Hermon Christian Writers Conference—those on staff and those who volunteer, those on faculty and those serving in innumerable other roles—thank you. Over the past decade, I can trace virtually every milestone on my journey as an author back to something amazing God did at Mount Hermon. You are truly making a difference for the kingdom!

And to you, dear reader: How can I ever thank you enough for allowing me to serve you through this work? You have many choices, and I am deeply humbled that you would choose to read this study. May our heavenly Father bless you as you journey through His wonderful Word.

Most of all, my heart is overflowing with gratitude to my loving Lord and King. I am nothing apart from Him and have nothing to offer apart from His grace working in my life. Thank you, Jesus, for calling me out of the darkness and into Your glorious Light. To Your Name alone belongs all glory, honor, and praise!

ABOUT THE AUTHOR

SHADIA HRICHI IS A PASSIONATE BIBLE teacher, multi-award-winning author, and speaker who has a heart for seeing lives transformed by the power of God's Word. Having experienced much heartache, such as a broken home, abortion, and divorce, Shadia captures the hearts of her audience as she illustrates God's love, faithfulness, and power of redemption through her personal experience.

She has received a master's in biblical and theological studies from Western Seminary, as well as a master's in criminal justice from the State University of New York. Shadia is the author of several Bible studies, including *Tamar*, *Hagar*, *Rahab*, *Ruth*, and *Worthy of Love*, a story-driven Bible study for post-abortion healing. In addition to teaching Bible studies, Shadia is often invited to speak at churches, conferences, women's retreats, and other events. Her insightful, witty, yet vulnerable teaching style reveals a compassion for the hurting, love for Jesus, and uncompromising commitment to the truth of God's Word.

Currently residing in Northern California, Shadia loves to visit the ocean each week for "a date with Jesus." Be sure to visit www.shadiahrichi.com and join Shadia's email community to access your free gifts, including Bible Study Tips, How to Plan a Sabbath Date with Jesus, Sneak Peeks into her writing, and lots of other free resources. *Legion* is the second study in her *Behind the Seen* series, centered on a story that serves as a beautiful reminder that God is always working *behind the seen*. Be among the first to be notified of the next study!

ABOUT THE STUDY

WELCOME, FRIEND! YOU ARE IN FOR AN ADVENTURE. THE story of Tamar, with all its sordid twists and turns, could not be a more fitting place to embark on a journey of *Rediscovering the God Who Redeems Me.*

This book is divided into six weeks, each comprising five days of personal study. For added flexibility, choose a commitment level that works best for you: "light" (15 minutes/day), "moderate" (30 minutes/day), "in-depth" (45 minutes/day), or "all-in" (60 minutes/day). See Group Study Tips (on the next page) for more details.

Each day of study includes one or more questions suitable for group discussion. These questions are followed by a . Be sure not to overlook these questions, even if you are working through the material on your own. There are also Pause to Ponder sections throughout the study; these are designed to provide you with a time of personal reflection. Use the space in the margin (or, if you prefer, a journal or notebook) to respond to these questions. For readers desiring to dig even deeper, I've prepared Extra questions, which are preceded by a . In addition to this workbook, optional video teaching sessions are available at www.shadiahrichi.com.

At the end of each day, there is a Your Turn section for personal application. These questions are very important. While studying the Bible can stir our hearts and open our eyes to wonderful truths, only when we apply what we have learned will it have a lasting impact for God's kingdom. In addition to this workbook, optional video teaching sessions are available at www.shadiahrichi.com/legion.

During my exploration of this story, I often found myself fascinated by secondary topics related to the material. The Supplemental Readings I've included throughout the study are not essential, but you may find them enjoyable and informative. If you are doing the study as a group, one of the biggest challenges can be accommodating different time constraints among individual participants. For this purpose, I have included a section called Group Study Tips, which you may find useful.

One quick note: some paraphrase versions of the Bible may be inadequate for the purposes of this study. Whenever possible, it is recommended that you complete the exercises using a Bible translation that adheres to a more literal translation, such as the English Standard Version, New American Standard Bible, New King James Version, or King James Version.

Before you begin, take a few moments to ask the Holy Spirit to guide you over the next six weeks and to bless your commitment to this study. Then, as you open your Bible and your heart, begin each day with an eager expectation of *Rediscovering the God Who Rescues Me*.

GROUP STUDY TIPS

BECAUSE ANY DEEP WORK OF GOD REQUIRES A SACRIFICE of time spent in His Word and in His presence, the volume of material in an in-depth study can be challenging for some participants. For this reason, several suggestions are provided to help you facilitate the study when participants have varying levels of time constraints.

Video Teaching Sessions

Seven optional video teaching sessions serve to complement and enhance the study. Watch Session One before you begin. Then, watch Session Two through Session Six before completing Week Two through Week Six in the study. Finally, as a wrap-up, watch Session Seven when you finish the study. Session One is approximately 15 minutes; the other sessions run for 20–25 minutes. Video sessions are available at www.shadiahrichi.com/.

Plan an Extended Schedule

Instead of meeting for six weeks, allow two weeks for each chapter, for a total of twelve weeks. Every other week, invite participants to watch and discuss Shadia's video teaching sessions. These modifications will also provide periodic opportunities for participants to "catch up" on anything they may have missed or to spend extra time on areas of the study they may wish to explore further.

Customized Commitments for a Six-Week Schedule

Based on a six-week format, the following are suggested assignments based on an individual's time constraints.

For All Participants

- Read through each day's material, including the assigned Bible passages.
- Optional: read the Supplemental Reading section as provided in various weeks.

Light (15 minutes a day)

- Complete the Your Turn personal application section at the end of each day.
- If you have time, complete the Group Discussion questions identified with a .

Moderate (30 minutes a day)

- Complete the various Pause to Ponder personal reflection sections as well as the Your Turn personal application section at the end of each day.
- Complete the Group Discussion questions identified with a .

In-Depth (45 minutes a day)

- Complete all questions except for the Extra questions identified with a .

All-In (60 minutes a day)

- Complete all questions, including the Extra questions identified with a .
- Read all the Supplemental Reading sections.

May the Lord bless you as you journey through this study!

A NOTE FROM THE AUTHOR

If there is one universal truth, it is that every human heart longs for paradise: a perfect world without death, pain, or sorrow. A world at peace, where each of us is secure, treasured, and loved. But the reality is that the world as we know it will never deliver; *it cannot*. Scripture tells us that "the whole world lies in the power of the evil one" (1 John 5:19).

As a result, you and I live in a broken world—a world that has been drifting off course ever since that slippery serpent enticed our first parents to reject God's authority in that garden paradise so long ago. In that moment, they unwittingly handed over dominion of the earth to Satan on a silver platter. But this then begs the question: *Why was God willing to risk rebellion in the Garden? And why would God allow His perfect creation to fall victim to the enemy's schemes? And if God is good, why does He allow evil to exist?*

Over the next six weeks, you and I will explore the answers to these questions and more as we step into the fascinating story of the man known only by the name of the demons that tormented him. To be honest, I don't know why I am attracted to the hard stories in the Bible—the messy stories. I suspect it stems, in part, from my own broken past. I can relate much easier to the broken people—the ones who experienced times when they felt unseen, or unloved, or unwanted. At the same time, their stories captivate my heart because when God reveals what He is doing *behind the seen*, His power and glory are displayed in ways that make my spirit soar!

So I invite you to come with me as we climb into the boat with Jesus and head into enemy territory. We will witness Jesus's power and passion as He battles violent storms and armies of demons in order to rescue . . . *one . . . lost . . . soul.*

Tormented, chained, and living in a graveyard, the man had no one to help him—no one to intercede for him. No one but Jesus. As a result of Jesus's pursuit:

- A demoniac becomes a disciple.
- A house of demons becomes a dwelling for the Living God.
- The chained becomes a champion of good news.

You and I live in a world crying out for rescue. And just as Jesus was willing to cross the sea and rescue one man from the enemy's chains, He crossed the heavens to rescue you and me from a fate even worse: *eternal chains*. But praise God that through His sacrifice for sin, Jesus conquered all the forces of evil and opened up the gates of paradise to all who embrace His mercy. So come with me; let's rediscover the God Who Rescues Me!

Your sister in Christ,

Shadia

"For He rescued us from the domain of darkness,
and transferred us to the kingdom of His beloved Son."
—Colossians 1:13 NASB

PART I

THE BONDAGE

NOTES

WEEK ONE

REFLECTING ON GOD'S RISK

WE ARE NOT EVEN TOLD HIS NAME: THE MAN OTHERWISE known by the demons that tormented him—Legion. The Gospel writers simply describe him as a "demoniac." If there is one story in the New Testament that epitomizes the ravages of evil in humanity, it has to be the story we are going to explore over the next six weeks as we journey through the Gospel of Mark.

But before we begin in Mark, a question begs to be answered: If God, who is infinite and all-knowing, knew of all the pain, chaos, and suffering that evil would inflict on His beloved children, then why did He allow sin to enter the world in the first place?

DAY ONE

Pondering Our Divine Design

"It was a dark and stormy night . . ." This famous opening line from *Paul Clifford* powerfully sets the stage for an intriguing story, but the concept didn't originate there. In fact, the scene is exactly how the story of Legion begins: "When evening had come, [Jesus] said to them, 'Let us go across to the other side.' . . . And a great windstorm arose, and the waves were breaking into the boat" (Mark 4:35, 37).

It's dark. A storm is raging. The waters are out of control. Even these seasoned fishermen will soon begin to panic in the chaos. But I'm getting ahead of myself. It is a remarkable story, and it's one I cannot wait for us to dive into. However, to properly study any passage in the Bible, we must first consider how the passage fits within the book in which it appears, as well as how it all fits within the Bible as a whole. This helps us to set the stage for whatever passage we are studying. So before we open Mark's Gospel and dive into the details of our story, we will spend a few days exploring the events that begin with the Bible's first mention of darkness, untamed waters, and chaos.

"The earth was without form and void, and darkness was over the face of the deep. And the Spirit of God was hovering over the face of the waters."
—Genesis 1:2

In the Beginning

Perhaps you are already familiar with the major events recorded in the first three chapters of Genesis:

- God creates the world in six days; He rests on the seventh day.
- God creates Adam and Eve, to whom He gives authority over the earth and all its creatures.
- Adam and Eve live in a garden paradise, enjoying God's presence.
- Then one day, a snake talks, Eve listens, Adam bites, and it all falls apart.

Did God know the risk in allowing humanity to sin and forfeit their dominion over the earth? Of course He did. From our limited perspective, the events in Genesis appear risky; but for God, this divine risk sets the stage for a glorious *divine rescue*.

The original meaning of the word cosmos, from the Greek *kosmos*, is "order" and "harmony," and only later did it come to be synonymous with "universe."

From Chaos to Cosmos

Read Genesis 1:1–25. How is the earth described according to verse 2?

This passage is packed with contrasts. Fill in the following blanks based on these contrasts. I completed one as an example.

God shines ________________ into the darkness.

He establishes *order* out of chaos.

Out of emptiness, He ________________ the earth with life.

Pause to Ponder

Consider the three statements you completed. Try to imagine if one or more of these aspects were missing in our world. Would you still be able to enjoy it? Explain.

Record your thoughts in the margin; do this for all Pause to Ponder sections.

Just imagine a world that is orderly and full of life, but without any light to behold it. Or a world full of light and life, but without any order: no assurance of another sunrise, or seasons, or any physical laws to help us make sense of our world. It is by His wisdom and kindness that God brings light, order, and a world filled with creatures into being *before* He brings humanity—the crown of His creation—to enter and enjoy it.

Read Genesis 1:26–31. In addition to God's blessing "be fruitful and multiply," what else does God tell Adam and Eve to do? Describe this responsibility in your own words.

"The heavens are the LORD's heavens, but the earth he has given to the children of man."
—Psalm 115:16

Regarding man's relation to the earth, the verb commonly translated "subdue" is from the Hebrew root word *kabash*. This verb is quite severe; it literally means to make into a slave. In other words, God expects humanity to exercise kingly authority over the earth, to care for it as God's trusted stewards, and to enjoy its benefits. Humans, created in the image of God, are the only creatures who are given delegated authority. We have been assigned with caring for the earth and all of its creatures. That's quite a responsibility! And yet this delegated authority is a beautiful invitation for humanity to share in God's wonderful work.

Pause to Ponder

In your opinion, how has humanity responded to this responsibility? Where would you place an X on the line below?

untrustworthy ——————————————— trustworthy

Explain your response.

"[Each day] we wake into a world we didn't make, into a salvation we didn't earn."[1]
—Eugene H. Peterson

A Sabbath Rest

If there is one thing my friends know about me, it is that I set aside one day each week for a date with Jesus. But this was not always so. It took a near crash and burn incident to teach me the importance of God's design for regular rest. I hate to confess it, but the lesson occurred while I was in seminary. It was not a class or a textbook that drove the message home, though those were certainly provided. Rather, it was an increasingly frantic pace trying to juggle a job, write papers, attend classes, and honor other commitments and responsibilities.

Seven days went by without taking a break, then eight, then nine . . . ten . . . eleven. Each day, I reasoned I could push through one more day. Just one more paper. One more task. One more late night at the computer. Until one day, I finally pushed it too far. I crashed. I was so physically and mentally exhausted that I spent the following week in bed, too ill to do anything at all. Several months later, one of my seminary professors had his class read an article called "The Pastor's Sabbath" by Eugene H. Peterson. God used Peterson's wise words to help me recognize that God's design for a weekly day of rest is a *gift!* It's an opportunity for extended communion with our Creator and to be reminded that "apart from [Him we] can do nothing" (John 15:5). I share some ideas on planning a Sabbath day at the end of this study.

God's design for a weekly day of rest is a *gift!*

Read Genesis 2:1–3. What did God do on the seventh day and why?

When you think of a Sabbath day (or day of rest), what comes to mind? How would you describe it?

This is the first time we read of God bestowing a blessing over something other than His creatures. The words "the seventh day" are mentioned a full three times in just two verses; clearly, the author wants his audience to take notice.

Read Exodus 16:23, 29–30. Compare these verses with Genesis 2:2–3. What similarities can you discover?

Using a Bible dictionary or conventional dictionary, define the word "holy."

Reflect on your description of a Sabbath rest. Does the concept of the Sabbath day being holy impact your understanding of God's design for rest? Explain.

Although a formal command to observe a Sabbath rest was not established by God until Exodus 16, the concept of Sabbath, a day of rest, originates from the Hebrew verb *shabath* in Genesis 2. This word suggests simply stopping or taking a break rather than recovery from hard work.

Read Isaiah 40:28 in the margin and John 5:17 in your Bible. In what ways can you take comfort in knowing that God never wearies or stops working?

"The LORD is the everlasting God, the Creator of the ends of the earth. He does not faint or grow weary."
—Isaiah 40:28

The reality is that if God stopped working, the universe would instantly fall apart. Scripture teaches that He holds all things together (Col. 1:17; see also Rom. 11:36). When we read that God rested, it serves as an example to follow, as well as a foreshadowing of a greater rest yet to come. After God accomplished all He set out to do in creating the world, He took time to enjoy His creation—and He desires for us to enjoy it as well.

Consecrated by God

In Genesis 1:3–10, Scripture describes a number of incidents when God separated one thing from another. However, Genesis 2:3 is the first time something is set apart as consecrated, or holy, to God. And what does He consecrate? The light? The earth? Adam? No. He sets apart a period of time.

Glance back at Genesis 1:23, 26–27, and 31. On which day was humanity created?

In the Hebrew view of time, each day begins not in the morning but at sunset. "And there was evening and there was morning, the first day" (Gen. 1:5).

If Adam and Eve were the last creatures God made on the sixth day, on which day, then, did the first humans experience their first *full day* of life?

Do you think this is significant? Why or why not?

God worked for six days to create "the heavens and the earth . . . and all the host of them" (Gen. 2:1). His work on the sixth day included creating all the land animals and creatures. Then, when everything else was completed, He created humanity in His own image. This means that the first full day of humanity's existence was also the very first Sabbath day. It is not only the first day consecrated by God in the history of the world, but it foreshadows an even greater "rest" to come!

And He chose to share it with us!

Your Turn

When you consider God's establishment of a Sabbath, or day of rest, how do you tend to view it? A gift? A burden? A command to obey? Share your thoughts.

How often, on average, do you (either alone or with your spouse or family) set aside one day of the week for enjoying God's gifts of rest, His creation, and, most importantly, His presence?

every week

once or twice a month

I can't remember the last time I took a day off to simply enjoy God's presence

If you do regularly enjoy a day set apart for God, how has it impacted your relationship with God or helped you recognize your dependence on Him? Share your thoughts.

If you do not regularly enjoy a day set apart for God, or if you struggle to see the value in it, spend some time in prayer asking God to reveal to you His purpose in desiring His people to enjoy a day of "solemn rest, a holy Sabbath to the Lord" (Exod. 16:23). Write what He reveals to you.

Wherever you may be in this regard, take a moment and thank God for His desire to spend time with you. Write a prayer as He leads you.

Day Two
Falling for the Enemy's Charms

"And God saw everything that he had made, and behold, it was very good."

—Genesis 1:31

Let's pause here for just a moment. Scripture assures us that when God created the world, He "saw everything that he had made, and behold, it was very good." Yet when we consider all that is happening in our world today, the reality of those words can seem as far out of reach as the idyllic days of Eden itself. After all, people are suffering and have been for centuries. Wars. Disease. Human trafficking. Abortion . . . and the list goes on.

So what went wrong?

The First Garden Paradise

I confess, I don't like gardening. My late grandmother was a prolific gardener, as are my mother, aunt, and cousin. However, I am lucky if I can keep a cactus alive. Even my silk plants tremble when I walk by. Years ago, when I worked in an office and was leaving on vacation, I handed my one lonely plant to a coworker to care for while I was away. When I returned two weeks later, I not only failed to recognize the plant, but my coworker refused to return it, mumbling something about me not deserving to have one.

In Genesis 2:8, Scripture says that God planted a garden. In it, man would find everything he needed to enjoy life: delicious and nutritious food, plenty of fresh water, pleasant surroundings, immortality,[2] and, most importantly, the enjoyment of God's presence. But something entered in and was lurking in the shadows . . .

Read Genesis 2:15-17. (Optional: read Genesis 2:4-17.) What command and warning does God speak to Adam?

At this point, Adam had no frame of reference for the concepts of evil and death. On what basis, then, did God expect Adam to obey His command?

Pause to Ponder

> Think of a time when you struggled to understand something that God wanted you to do (or not do). What helped you move forward in obedience when what He required seemed to make no sense?

The Bait

In his commentary on the book of Genesis, Victor Hamilton explains, "There are only four chapters in the Bible where Satan is not present, the first two and the last two. The Bible begins and ends with him out of existence. But between Genesis 3 and Revelation 20 he is a factor to be reckoned with."[3]

Read Genesis 3:1–8; then, answer the questions that follow. (Optional: read Genesis 2:18–3:8.)[4]

Describe two or three things God could have done to prevent Adam and Eve from eating the forbidden fruit.

Do you find God's apparent inaction surprising? Confusing? Disturbing? Share your thoughts.

What reason(s) might God have had for choosing not to intervene? List as many as you can think of.

There are many ways God could have stepped in. He could have interrupted the serpent's conversation or prevented the serpent's access to the Garden altogether. God could have blocked the way to the tree by building a wall or posting an angel as a guard. One thing is clear: God could have stepped in if He wanted to. But He didn't.

If God had prevented the events leading up to Adam and Eve's disobedience, would these actions have removed Adam and Eve's ability to choose to disobey? Explain.

If God had stepped in, His involvement might have kept Adam and Eve's willingness to disobey hidden, but it could never remove the inherent vulnerability that existed from the start. While God made all things good, they were not made *unchangeably* good. God did not create evil; but from the beginning, He created humanity with the dignity of having freedom to make their own choices.

The Setup

Genesis 3:1 describes the serpent as being more crafty (or shrewd) than any other beast of the field that the Lord God had made.

Look up the word "crafty" in a dictionary and write the definition in your own words.

The Hebrew word for "crafty" in Scripture (*arum*) is neutral. Its interpretation, whether a positive trait (such as prudent) or negative (such as shrewd), depends on the context and the character of the one being described. We know that God made all creatures good (Gen. 1:31). However, the creatures were not all created the same. Each kind had a unique set of abilities and strengths. Perhaps the enemy's choice of the serpent as his instrument is not so surprising given that Jesus Himself describes the serpent as a wise creature (Matt. 10:16). Nevertheless, it is important to remember that both the serpent and the enemy speaking through it are created beings and are therefore infinitely inferior to the Almighty Creator of the universe.

Interesting fact: The origin of the word "universe" is the combination of "uni" (one) and "verse," which originates from the Latin *versus*, meaning a row or line of poetry. Our English word *universe* ("one verse"), therefore, affirms the biblical account of God speaking the world into existence with just one verse!

Contrast the serpent's remarks to Eve in Genesis 3:1 with the command God gave to Adam in Genesis 2:16–17. In what ways did the serpent twist God's words?

After implying that God was harsh and unkind by exaggerating His prohibition, the serpent then sat back and allowed the woman to correct him. Although Eve

corrected the exaggeration—even defending God's goodness—the serpent had successfully lured Eve into a deeper conversation.

The conversation moved to a discussion about God Himself. In fact, this was "the first conversation *about* God, the first religious, theological conversation"[5] in the Bible. The serpent began by claiming to have knowledge superior to God's. "You will surely not die." One scholar explains that because the serpent first removed the fear of penalty, the victim was primed to consider the benefits that would come from disobeying God's command.[6]

Pause to Ponder

When we dismiss God as harsh or unkind, are we afterward more susceptible to falling into temptation? Explain.

How can knowing and trusting in God's Word make you less vulnerable to the enemy's attacks?

The Fall

Genesis 3:6 states that Adam was with Eve; however, it is unclear whether he was with her during the conversation with the serpent, or whether the events beginning in verse 6 occurred later. However, Scripture does not indicate that Eve left the serpent to go and find Adam.

Consider again Genesis 3:1-8; then, answer the questions that follow. Apart from taking the fruit right then and there, what else could Eve have done?

What else could Adam have done?

What principle can you apply to your own life?

The serpent never actually told Eve to eat the fruit. In the same way, Eve never actually told Adam to eat the fruit. As a matter of fact, whether the serpent remained on the scene after he spoke to Eve is not clear. However, the seed of doubt of

God's goodness had been planted. From there, the temptation slithered almost effortlessly into human consciousness.

Glance back at Genesis 1:27–28. What authority did God delegate to Adam and Eve?

Being that the serpent is also one of God's creatures, how did Adam and Eve respond to their delegated authority?

Sadly, rather than ruling over the creatures as God had intended, Adam and Eve allowed a creature to rule over them. In effect, they turned God's created order upside down.

Read John 12:31–32 and Ephesians 2:1–2. Describe Satan according to these verses.

In what ways do these descriptions shed light on what we are studying?

By bowing to Satan's words instead of God's, Adam and Eve handed Satan their delegated authority on a silver platter.[7] As a result, Satan became the new "ruler of this world."

Read Job 1:6–12 and 2:1–6. Whom must Satan answer to?

In what ways can you take comfort in knowing that all authority ultimately belongs to God?

Half-Truths

After casting doubt on God's goodness, the serpent suggested that God had selfish motives for His threats. The serpent made three specific promises.

In the table below, list the three promises Satan made in Genesis 3:4–5 in the order they appear in the passage. Then, next to each one, state whether or not the promise was confirmed. I completed the first one for you.

Promise	Outcome (Did the serpent's words come true?)
1. *You will not die.*	*Yes*
2.	
3.	*(Hint: read Gen. 3:22)*

Ponder the table. What conclusions can you draw?

The serpent was crafty indeed. It appears he was correct; however, his words were only half-truths. First, Adam and Eve did not die in that moment, but God's warning of death would soon come to pass. Second, their eyes were opened, but rather than bringing happiness, wisdom, and power, it brought consciousness of sin and the resulting fear and shame. Finally, the serpent's promise—you will be like God, knowing good and evil—was confirmed, in one sense, by God Himself in Genesis 3:22. However, the "knowing" was not on a level that brought them closer to God. In fact, it sent them cowering into the shadows away from His presence.

"But each person is tempted when he is lured and enticed by his own desire."
—James 1:14

Read James 1:14 in the margin. What insight does this verse offer in light of the events we are studying?

Read James 4:7 and 1 Peter 5:8-9. In what manner should a Christian respond to the enemy's schemes, according to these verses?

Like every human being who would follow them, Adam and Eve each had a choice to make: God's will or my will? Asserting self-will when it is in conflict with God's will is always disobedience, which is sin. As with Eve, the danger for each of us is not when we take the first bite (by then, it's too late), but when we *engage* with the enemy in conversation. To this day, he whispers his deception into any receptive ears: "Did God really say . . . ?"

Your Turn

Thinking on your past, in what ways has the enemy attempted to cast doubt on:

God's goodness in your heart and mind?

The authority of God's Word in your life?

How about right now? Is there an area of your life in which you are tempted to doubt God's goodness or downplay the teaching in God's Word? If so, bring the situation to God in prayer and ask Him to help you see what might be at the root of your struggle. Write a prayer in response to what God reveals to you.

Whether or not you are experiencing this kind of struggle right now, what one thing can you do this week to guard your heart and mind from the enemy's schemes? Write a prayer of response below.

Day Three
Clothed in God's Mercy

One afternoon when I was around five years old, I was exploring in our family's garage. Being curious, I opened various doors and drawers just to see what was inside. When I pulled on the handle of a particularly large drawer, the weight of its contents quickly overpowered my little-girl strength. In an instant, the drawer fell forward, spilling a silver sea of nuts, bolts, and hardware all over the garage floor. Glancing to my right and left, I quickly scurried away, hoping no one would notice. Later, when my parents confronted me about it, I did what any typical five-year-old would do: I blamed it on my baby brother.

Did you ever try to shift the blame when you were a child? Surely I am not the only one. Perhaps you pointed your finger at a sibling, the neighbor's kid . . . grandpa? Sadly, it seems that no one needs to teach children how to blame; blame has been around since the Garden of Eden.

"Eden" in Hebrew means "delight" or "happiness." It is not the name of the garden, but rather the country or region where God planted His garden.[8]

The Blame Game

Read Genesis 3:8–13 (verse 8 is review). The passage shows God taking initiative; what do we learn about God's character?

In Genesis 3:9, God asks Adam, "Where are you?" (Note: "you" is singular in Genesis 3:9 and 11.) Since God knows everything, why might God have asked Adam this question?

God knew Adam was hiding, but rather than offering condemnation, God gently coaxed Adam out of hiding. His patient questioning was intended to lead Adam to a place of restoration. One scholar writes, "In love and mercy God searched after His fallen creatures with the question 'Where are you?' This question proved two things—that man was lost and that God had come to seek. It proved man's sin and God's grace. God takes the initiative in salvation, demonstrating the very thing Satan got Eve to doubt—His love."[9]

What reason did Adam give for being afraid in Genesis 3:10?

Do you find Adam's response curious or surprising? Explain.

> "God's kindness is meant to lead you to repentance."
> —Romans 2:4

I don't know about you, but I find it curious that, rather than confessing he was afraid because he disobeyed God's command, Adam told God that he was afraid because he was naked. After all, Adam had been naked since day one. Yet being naked is the reason he gave for hiding from God. The internal guilt resulted in an immediate feeling of external shame and an attempt to try to cover himself. However, even there, right from the start, we see God's mercy and kindness at work. Romans 2:4 teaches, "God's kindness is meant to lead you to repentance."

The kindness of God that the serpent sought to cast doubt on was the very kindness that invited Adam to enter God's presence and confess his disobedience.

Consider the text carefully. Who does Adam ultimately blame for his disobedience? (Circle one)

Himself   Eve   God   Serpent

Read Proverbs 19:3 in the margin and Psalm 37:23-24 in your Bible. Describe these principles in your own words. Include both a warning and a promise in your description.

"When a man's folly brings his way to ruin, his heart rages against the LORD." —Proverbs 19:3

Here is Adam's chance, but instead of reaching out to God and admitting his guilt, Adam simultaneously threw Eve under the bus and blamed God: "This woman *you* gave me . . ." How this must have delighted that slippery serpent. He not only succeeded in introducing hostility between Adam and Eve, as well as division between God and humanity, but on top of that, *God got blamed for it all!*

Pause to Ponder

Describe a time you did something wrong and then shifted the blame onto someone else (even if you shifted the blame only in your mind). What were the results?

How can shifting the blame onto someone else injure your relationship with God?

Ever since the Garden, our enemy has been lurking in the shadows of our lives, looking for ways to drive a wedge between ourselves and others and between ourselves and God. The hostility between Adam and Eve eventually passed on to their sons, and from them to all generations. From the beginning, the world has suffered at the enemy's schemes—an enemy who delights in hostility, division, and rebellion against God. Perhaps most tragic of all is that his weapon of choice is *us*.

If the enemy can convince us that others are to blame—that others are the enemy—we are playing right into his hands. This doesn't mean that people are never accountable for their actions, but we often fail to recognize how the enemy has been inflicting havoc on the human race since the beginning. The reality is that people are not the enemy; rather, they are slaves of the enemy.

People are not the enemy; rather, they are slaves of the enemy.

In Genesis 3:13, God asked Eve a question. What was her response?

Identify the ways Eve's response in Genesis 3:13 is similar to Adam's in Genesis 3:12. In what ways is it different?

While Eve follows Adam's example of pointing blame, she merely presents a statement of fact: "The serpent deceived me, and I ate." Now, at last, the underlying source of rebellion is exposed.

The Curse

Read Genesis 3:14–19. Who or what is cursed?

Who or what is *not* cursed? Does this surprise you? Why or why not?

Adam may have been so called because he was taken from the *adamah* ("cultivated ground" in Hebrew), which he would cultivate in life and return to in death.[10]

In contrast to God's dealing with Adam, God did not engage the serpent in conversation but rather cursed him right from the start. His outright rebellion and blatant deceit provided no opportunity for confession, no possibility for redemption. Adam and Eve, however, were not cursed, but rather punished (or disciplined) for disobeying God's command. Here again, we see God's grace in action. While Adam and Eve would experience hardship, pain, strife, and eventually death—even in death there is still hope.

The Promise

Thankfully, God was not finished. God went on to speak a prophecy hinting at an ultimate victory over that slippery serpent.

Glance once more at Genesis 3:15–19. When does God announce His promise of deliverance: before pronouncing judgment on Adam and Eve or after?

before after

Do you find this sequence of events encouraging? Surprising? Share your thoughts.

Within one little verse (v. 15), we find the promise of deliverance for the entire human race. This verse, like the full passage of Genesis 3:14–19, is both poetic and prophetic in form, which can make it more challenging to interpret. However, when we examine it through the lens of the New Testament, the picture becomes clearer. Let's take a brief look at a passage in Romans to help us shed some light on this prophecy.

Read Romans 1:7 and 16:20.

Who is the letter written to?

What assurances are given to the recipients?

Now, read Romans 16:17–19.

How does the context provide further insight into Romans 16:20?

God's promise of victory over the enemy, spoken to Adam and Eve so long ago, is now coming into focus. Our enemy is not a physical creature but a spiritual one—that is, Satan. Nevertheless, he is still a creature and therefore infinitely inferior to the One who created him. From the beginning, the Creator of the universe, God Almighty, has assured us that the enemy will one day be defeated. But until then, God has His own reasons for the delay.

"The Lord is not slow to fulfill his promise as some count slowness, but is patient toward you, not wishing that any should perish, but that all should reach repentance."
—2 Peter 3:9

Read 2 Peter 3:9 in the margin; then, answer the questions that follow.

What is God's desire?

Is anyone excluded?

Describe how you have experienced or witnessed this truth personally.

The Hope

Read Genesis 3:20–24. What reason is given for Adam's choice to name his wife Eve?

What does Adam's name choice suggest about his outlook on the future?

Adam named his wife Eve (pronounced "Haw-wah" in Hebrew, which sounds like the word for "life"). They had no children at this point. Not only that, God had announced that death was in their future. But Adam still had a choice. Despite God's pronouncement of hardship, pain, decay, and death, Adam chose to hold on to one glimmer of hope: God's promise that deliverance would one day come through the offspring (or seed) of the woman.

Describe all the ways God extended mercy to Adam and Eve, based on Genesis 3:20–24.

By making garments of skins for Adam and Eve, God showed mercy and kindness even in the midst of His pronouncement of judgment. God was both just and merciful. While sin against a holy God must be punished, He provided a temporary covering until sin was dealt with once and for all. God could have spoken garments into existence from thin air as He did all the rest of creation. He could have used wool, cotton, or flax, but covering Adam and Eve's nakedness required more than these.

Read Leviticus 17:11 and Hebrews 9:22.

What does God require to atone for sin, according to these verses?

What do these verses reveal about God's view of sin?

God as Creator

There are many ways God could have introduced Himself in Genesis 1:1. He could have revealed Himself as Law-Giver, God Almighty, or even Father, but He did not. He chose to introduce Himself as Creator. "In the beginning, *God created* . . ." God is the Author of Life itself. Because God is also compassionate, kind, and merciful, having to slaughter one of His innocent creatures would have been deeply painful to His holy heart. However, for God to take this action, there must have been a heartache even more painful that the slaughter averted.

Your Turn

How does the fact that God was willing to shed innocent blood to "cover" humanity's sin speak to you personally?

Do you sense God calling, "Where are you?" Is there sin in your life that you need to confess? If so, turn to the God of mercy who loves you and is calling to you. Spend some time in prayer and write what God reveals to you.

Ponder all the ways God has extended mercy to you over the past week. Write a prayer of gratitude in response to what He reveals to you.

Day Four
Recognizing My Captivity

"Thou hast made us for thyself, O Lord, and our heart is restless until it finds its rest in thee."
—Saint Augustine, *Confessions*

When we last read of Adam and Eve, they had been banished from the Garden and God's presence—a painful homelessness of body *and* spirit. While the banishment broke Adam and Eve's communion with God, even there we see evidence of God's mercy.

Glance back at Genesis 3:22-24. What did God do to keep Adam and Eve away from the Tree of Life?

What could God have done instead?

So often when we read of God's discipline, we tend to focus on the misery and pain it causes, when in fact it is always a picture of God's mercy and grace. By keeping the couple away from the Tree of Life, God ensured that Adam and Eve would not live for all eternity plagued by sin, guilt, and shame.

God could have simply destroyed the tree, but He did not. It stands as His eternal promise that there is still hope. By allowing Adam and Eve many years in which to grow, learn, seek God, and repent, He extended the hope of reconciliation. Nevertheless, their descendants would suffer the effects of sin for generations.

Prepare the Way of the Lord

Fast-forward to the New Testament era. People have suffered for centuries. Famines. Wars. Disease. Slavery. By the time Jesus arrived on the scene, God's people, the

Jews, had been under Roman rule for nearly one hundred years and were suffering under all kinds of strongholds: sin, slavery, disease, demon-possession, legalism. Anxious for deliverance, they were eagerly awaiting their Messiah.

What types of strongholds are people suffering under in the world today? List as many as you can think of.

Read Mark 1:1–8. What message does John the Baptist proclaim to the people?

What comes to mind when you think of repentance?

The average English dictionary defines repentance as feeling deep sorrow or regret. In the biblical sense, however, to repent of something involves emotion *followed by action*. Specifically, it assumes remorse over one's sin that causes the person to "change his mind" and "to turn around." In other words, repentance is to *turn from* sin and to *follow after* God. However, when God is removed from the equation, hope is lost and only sorrow remains.

The call for repentance is a call for us to return to our "creaturely (and covenant) dependence on God." —J. D. G. Dunn

When John the Baptist began preaching in the wilderness, he expected the people to take action along with their confession. The people not only confessed their sins, but they were baptized, symbolizing their recognition of the need for cleansing from sin. Repentance is "a decisive act of turning from the old way of life and a throwing oneself on the mercy of the Coming One . . . [calling us to return to our] creaturely (and covenant) dependence on God."[11]

Pause to Ponder

Reread the quote in the margin. How does it shed light on your understanding of repentance?

Apart from Christ, in Me Dwells No Good Thing

"You will always be my friend . . . You know too much." These are the words written on a favorite coffee mug given to me by a dear friend. I smile whenever I see it, but to be honest, I shudder at what I am capable of apart from the grace of God.

The words of legendary author and preacher Oswald Chambers express it best: "If the Spirit of God has given you a vision of what you are apart from the grace of God . . . you know there is no criminal who is half so bad in actuality as you know yourself to be in possibility."[12]

The apostle Paul reminds us in Romans 7:18, "For I know that nothing good dwells in me, that is, in my flesh." The reality is that we are all sinners in need of God's grace. Apart from Him, in each of us dwells *no good thing*.

The Time Is Fulfilled

Read Mark 1:9–15. Rewrite the events in verses 9–11 using your own words.

"Oh, that you would rend the heavens and come down . . . come down to make your name known to your enemies."

—Isaiah 64:1–2 NIV

Describe anything about Mark's description of Jesus's baptism that you find interesting or striking.

Mark's use of vivid imagery to describe the events surrounding Jesus's baptism is not accidental. Regarding Jesus coming up out of the water, Mark writes that the heavens were "torn open." The verb Mark uses depicts a forceful or violent tearing apart or division. The root verb is *schizo* in Greek, which simply means "to split." Right from the start, Mark is painting a picture for his readers using words that convey a sense of urgency, force, and even violence. Keep this in mind as we move ahead through his Gospel.

The Kingdom of God Is at Hand

After Jesus's baptism and Satan's temptations, Jesus begins His ministry.[13]

Complete Jesus's message in Mark 1:15 by filling in the blanks. (Note: some paraphrase versions of the Bible may not work for this exercise.)

The time is ______________.

The kingdom of God is ______________.

Repent and believe in the ______________.

"But when the fullness of time had come, God sent forth his Son, born of woman." —Galatians 4:4

Read Galatians 4:4 in the margin. What might "the fullness of time" mean? List two or three possibilities.

One commentary author writes,

> The sending of Christ in the fullness of time refers not so much to world conditions in the sense that the prevalence of Greek as a common spoken language, Roman roads, and the Roman enforced peace made the rapid spread of the gospel possible. Rather the emphasis is on God whose sending of Christ is not a "last-ditch effort," but part of God's gracious plan from the beginning.[14]

The fullness of time, then, tells us that God had already set the time as He Himself determined, irrespective of any outside conditions. In other words, God's agenda and timeline are not dependent on anything—He sent Jesus precisely when He determined to do so long ago. What a precious comfort and reminder! God never reacts to anything. He is and was and always will be in complete control.

"[Jesus] was foreknown before the foundation of the world but was made manifest in the last times for the sake of you." —1 Peter 1:20

Jesus announces in Mark 1:15 that "the kingdom of God is at hand." How might this news have been understood by Jesus's hearers? List two or three possibilities.

Jesus's arrival did not usher in the kingdom of God in the way people had hoped. The Jewish people at that time expected their Messiah to conquer Rome and set up an earthly kingdom in its place. At the other end of the spectrum, people in our day often perceive the kingdom of God as heaven, a future experience and distant place far out of reach. Both of these perspectives miss the point.

There is one thing that sets a kingdom apart from all other forms of rule or government: a king. It is the presence and authority of a king that makes a kingdom. The kingdom of God, then, requires a King who embodies the presence and authority of God Himself. As such, it is unlike any other kingdom on earth.

Reread Mark 1:1. Describe how Mark introduces his Gospel.

The word "Christ" (*Christos* in Greek) denotes "king." The word literally means "Anointed One." Because Jewish kings were anointed with oil, the word "anointed" (or *Christos*) became synonymous with king.

How does the meaning of the word "Christ" add further depth to Jesus's words "the kingdom of God is at hand"?

The kingdom of God being near means that the *King* is near.

From the start, Mark presents Jesus as the Christ—that is, the King. The kingdom of God being near means that the *King* is near. Not just any king, but *the* King! Psalm 24 is perhaps the most beautiful prophecy concerning this coming king. You may enjoy meditating on this psalm when you have some time.

Repent and Believe in the Gospel

Then we reach the last part of Jesus's message in Mark 1:15: "repent and believe in the gospel." The word "gospel" is *euangelion* in Greek. The word is derived from the verb *euaggelizo*, which simply means to bring or announce good news.

"I have set my King on Zion, my holy hill." —Psalm 2:6

Since Jesus had just begun His ministry, what might "the gospel" have meant to the people at this point in time?

Read Acts 19:4. According to the apostle Paul, the message of John the Baptist was twofold: to call the people to repentance and (fill in the blanks):

"to ________________ in the one who was to come after him, that is, ________________."

"Messiah" and "Christ" both mean anointed, which signifies kingship. Messiah comes from the Hebrew word *mashiach*, meaning anointed one.[15]

All four Gospel writers introduce John the Baptist as being the messenger prophesied by Isaiah as crying out in the wilderness to "prepare the way of the Lord." Simply put, John the Baptist is telling the people that the Lord—the Messiah—is coming. However, when Jesus arrives bringing *good news*, the Good News is the arrival of *Himself*. He is the long-awaited Messiah of God who, before setting up God's holy kingdom, comes to deal with what Adam lost in the Garden by taking away the sins of the world (John 1:29).

You may have read or heard the Good News previously or maybe this is the first time. While the message is for everyone, the call is personal. Jesus came to earth to give His life as a ransom by taking our punishment for sins on the cross so that we would not spend eternity separated from God (see Mark 10:45 and 1 Tim. 2:6). He invites each one of us to embrace this gift by turning from our old life and following Him as our Lord. Have you acknowledged and repented of your sin and embraced Jesus Christ, the Son of God, as your personal Lord and Savior?

You can respond to His marvelous gift right now by asking God to forgive your sins and committing to follow Jesus as the Lord of your life from this day forward. God promises in His Word: "In [Jesus] we have redemption through his blood, the forgiveness of our trespasses, according to the riches of his grace," for "God shows his love for us in that while we were still sinners, Christ died for us" (Eph. 1:7; Rom. 5:8). If you prayed this prayer, write your prayer in the margin with today's date. Then share your news with a friend, a group leader, or another member of the study. They'll be thrilled!

If you have already received God's gift of salvation, made possible only through the death and resurrection of Jesus Christ, write about the time and circumstances surrounding your experience in the margin. Follow it with a prayer of thanksgiving to God for His boundless love and faithfulness.

If you sense you need more time, ask God to bless your commitment to reading His Word and to help you be sensitive to His voice as you continue journeying through this study. We will explore this marvelous offer of salvation further in Week Five.

Your Turn

As we read at the beginning of today's lesson, when Jesus entered the world, the people were suffering under many strongholds: foreign rule, disease, sin, slavery, demon possession, legalism. Sadly, it is no different in our world today.

In what ways are you currently suffering under a stronghold? The stronghold may be overt (spiritual oppression or sinful activity) or less obvious (such as pride or legalism).

In what ways have you previously suffered under a stronghold?

Is there a stronghold that is currently blocking God's work from being exhibited in your life? If so, bring the matter to God in prayer. Write what He reveals to you, including any specific steps He wants you to take.

If you are not currently suffering any strongholds, write a prayer of gratitude for God's deliverance and protection.

Day Five
Acknowledging Jesus's Authority

At the beginning of his Gospel, Mark quickly moves through the ministry of John the Baptist, Jesus's baptism, Satan's temptations, Jesus's message, and Jesus calling his first disciples. Then Mark suddenly slows his pace as he begins to describe various dramatic events. We will explore several of these stories today; they will serve as a valuable framework as we move into the story of Legion in Week Two. Mark 1:21 begins with Jesus arriving in a village called Capernaum. It was the Sabbath and Jesus was teaching in the synagogue.

A New Teaching with Authority

A literary pattern called chiastic structure is common in Scripture, whereby the author intersects mirror images of words, concepts, or events in order to draw the reader's attention to what the author wants to emphasize. To help readers see the pattern, biblical scholars typically use pairs of letters (such as A with A^1, B with B^1) to identify parallel words, phrases, or concepts when outlining a chiastic structure.

Read Mark 1:22–27. (Optional: read verses 21 through 31.)

I've outlined verses 22–27 in their chiastic structure. Fill in the blanks with the appropriate word or phrase based on the text. I completed a few to get you started.

A The people were *astonished*
- **B** Jesus taught with __________
  - **C** Unclean spirit *cried out*
    - **D** Demon *challenges* Jesus
      - **E** Jesus is the __________ of God
    - **D^1** Jesus *silences* demon
  - **C^1** Unclean spirit __________
- **B^1** Jesus taught with *authority*

A^1 The people were *amazed*

As you can see, the idea in line A is similar to that in line A^1. The same is true for B and B^1 and so on. The author's goal is to draw our attention to the point where the parallels intersect—that is, the center of the chiasm. For this passage, the critical point that Mark wants his readers to recognize is this: Jesus is the Holy One of God. Everything surrounding this truth—Jesus teaching with authority, the demons crying out at His commands, the astonishment of the people—serves to affirm this glorious truth.

What reasons might Jesus have had for forbidding the demons from proclaiming the truth that He is the Holy One of God?

From the first words of Mark's Gospel through the beginning paragraphs, he focuses on one thing: Jesus is the Christ, the Son of God. As such, Jesus teaches *with authority*. By *His authority* He heals the sick (Mark 1:29–31). *His authority* silences demons and casts them out. While the people are amazed, wondering who Jesus is, the demons know exactly who Jesus is—and yet, Jesus forbids them to speak.

Theologian R. C. Sproul suggests that the demons assumed they would gain power over Jesus by revealing His identity before He had completed His mission.[16] One commentary author writes, "The popular idea of the Messiah was of a conquering king who . . . would blast the Romans and lead the Jews to world power. Therefore, if a rumor were to go out that the Messiah had arrived, the inevitable consequence would be rebellions and uprisings. . . . [N]othing but harm and trouble and disaster could come from the proclamation that the Messiah had arrived."[17]

However, "in God's economy, no fallen spirit could possibly have power over the second person of the Trinity, so the demons' shouting of Jesus' identity was pointless."[18] Nevertheless, the privilege of announcing Jesus as the Holy One of God would be reserved for worshipers, not blasphemers.

Read Mark 1:32–34. Why do you suppose the people came to Jesus at sundown? (Hint: glance back at verse 21.)

Consider our world today. Describe two or three religious barriers (apart from unrepentant sin) that hinder people from bringing their needs to God.

In what ways can you sympathize with the people in Jesus's day?

Jesus's Mission

By the time Jesus entered the world, the religious leaders had added hundreds and hundreds of rules to God's law. Rather than focusing on *changing hearts* to follow after God, their effort to protect the people from transgressing God's commands focused on *changing behavior*.

"No man knows how bad he is till he has tried very hard to be good."
—C. S. Lewis, *Mere Christianity*

Pause to Ponder

Read the quote in the margin. Do you agree? Have you ever experienced this firsthand? Share your thoughts.

Read Mark 1:38–39. (Optional: read verses 35–39.) Restate Jesus's mission according to verse 38.

Compare Jesus's stated mission in Mark 1:38 with what He actually does in verse 39. What conclusions can you draw? (Hint: reread 1:27.)

Jesus is on a mission. He has an important message to bring. The authority of His preaching is *confirmed* by His actions. "He commands even the unclean spirits, and they obey him" (Mark 1:27).

Read Mark 1:40–45.

What did Jesus tell the man to do, and how did the man respond?

How does the man's response in Mark 1:45 compare with the demon's response to Jesus's command in 1:25–26?

Does the man's disobedience surprise you? Share your thoughts.

In Jesus's day, lepers were forced to live as outcasts away from society. No one would dare touch a leper for fear of likewise becoming "unclean" (Lev. 13:45–46). Jesus could have healed the man with a word. Instead, being "moved with pity" (Mark 1:41), Jesus chose not only to heal, but to *touch* the leper. Jesus then "sternly

charged" the healed man not to tell anyone, but to go and show himself to the priest in accordance with Old Testament law (see Lev. 14). The phrase "sternly charged" (sometimes translated "strictly warned") is *embrimaomai* in Greek and conveys very strong emotion, such as scolding or admonishment. Nevertheless, despite Jesus's tender touch, miraculous healing, and stern warning, the man neither obeys Jesus nor seeks to follow Him.

Pause to Ponder

Have you (or someone you know) ever elevated an *experience* of God above the gift of God Himself? What dangers may lurk behind this motivation?

Glance back at Mark 1:45. In the table, fill in each blank with "Jesus" or "the leper." I completed the first one for you.

	Before leper is healed	After leper is healed
Who was hindered from moving freely within society?	*The leper*	
Who moved freely within society?		

Describe how this reversal speaks to you personally.

Friends Are a Gift from the Lord

Many years ago, when I was a baby Christian and still very emotionally guarded due to years of mental and emotional abuse, I met a new friend at church. After a year or more of gentle persistence, this friend managed to get past the walls I had built around my heart. Years later, as we were talking about this, I simply asked her, "How did you get in?" I will never forget her response: "I couldn't find any doors, and I couldn't find any windows, so I decided to climb the wall."

To this day, the memory of her words still makes me smile. I marvel at her tenacity in pursuing a friendship that she sensed was a gift from God. And while she and I encountered many trials along the way, our friendship remains strong because it is anchored in the Lord Jesus Christ.

Read Mark 2:1-7. Describe the barriers the friends faced and how far they were willing to go to bring the paralytic to Jesus.

Contrast what the friends hoped Jesus would do with what Jesus actually did. Do you find this curious or surprising? Share your thoughts.

Blessings and Curses

In Jewish culture at that time, sickness, disease, and poverty were often viewed as resulting from God's judgment for sin. In contrast, those who were wealthy and healthy were considered blessed and favored by God. This is due, in part, to numerous Old Testament principles and passages relating to blessings and curses. Sadly, the heart of the message was often neglected, eventually resulting in a twisted understanding of God's Word. As a result, the suffering of some of the people in Jesus's day was compounded by an unwarranted sense of condemnation and guilt.[19]

> "See, I am setting before you today a blessing and a curse: the blessing, if you obey the commandments of the LORD your God, which I command you today, and the curse, if you do not obey."
>
> —Deuteronomy 11:26-28

Finish the story by reading Mark 2:8-12 and Luke 5:25; then, answer the questions that follow. What reason does Jesus give for healing the man?

What significance might this have?

What does Jesus command the man to do after Jesus heals him, and how does the man respond?

Contrast the healed paralytic's obedience with the leper's disobedience in Mark 1:40-45. What might account for the difference? List as many reasons as you can think of.

It's a Trap!

Jesus demonstrates His authority over demons. He exhibits power over sickness. With a word, He heals even the most severe, permanent afflictions. He even assumes God's authority to forgive sins. From there, He dares to shatter the religious leaders' sacred traditions, proclaiming Himself to be lord of the Sabbath (Mark 2:23–28). In every way, Jesus exhibits divine authority. While His actions win the praise of many, they rouse indignation in others.

Read Mark 3:1-6. What offense did the religious rulers hope to catch Jesus committing?

Incredibly, the religious leaders (Pharisees) never disputed that Jesus had the power to heal. That was not their issue. Rather, they wanted to catch Jesus performing such an "offense" on the Sabbath—the day when *they* made the rules.

By what criteria does Jesus redefine what is lawful on the Sabbath? (Hint: see Mark 3:4.)

How does this compare with the religious leaders' view?

Glance back at Genesis 2:3. In your opinion, how well did the religious leaders seem to grasp God's original purpose for the Sabbath? Place an X on the line below.

not well ____________________________________ very well

Explain your response.

It is at this point in Mark's Gospel that we see the first signs of rebellion against Jesus. The religious leaders (Pharisees) and the political rulers (followers of Herod), previously at severe odds with one another, suddenly find common ground and join forces. Their aim? To destroy Jesus. The commoners, however, flock to Jesus.

Jesus's fame spread far and wide across the western region of the Jordan River. Many people traveled more than one hundred miles to reach Jesus (Mark 3:7–8).

Even people from foreign cities, such as Tyre and Sidon, came to Him. Bringing their sick, lame, and demon-possessed loved ones, they would be hoping against hope that what they heard of Jesus would be true.

Your Turn

Think back over the past few months. List all the ways you have been blessed by Jesus's authority in your life. Describe all the ways He has protected, healed, or guided you.

Where in your life right now do you need Jesus's authority? Consider the faith of the paralytic and his friends. What principles can you apply to your situation?

Think again over the past few months. Is there an area in your life that you habitually fail to surrender to Jesus's authority? What one step will you take this week to relinquish control? Write a prayer of commitment as God leads you.

Lesson Summary

What Scripture, statement, or thought was most significant to you this week? Write it down and then reword it into a prayer of response to God.

One thing I love to do at the end of each week's lesson is recommend a worship song. You can find the full playlist at www.shadiahrichi.com/bonus.

Notes

[1] Eugene H. Peterson, "The Pastor's Sabbath," *Christianity Today,* May 19, 2004.

[2] That is, by having unlimited access to the Garden's Tree of Life.

[3] Victor P. Hamilton, "Genesis," in *The Baker Illustrated Bible Commentary*, ed. Gary M. Burge and Andrew E. Hill (Grand Rapids, MI: Baker Book House, 2012), 12.

[4] A deeper exploration into the meaning of Eve being built from Adam's side and the fascinating parallel concept of the building of God's temple can be found in my Bible study *Hagar: Rediscovering the God Who Sees Me* (Abilene, TX: Leafwood Publishers, 2017).

[5] Dietrich Bonhoeffer, *Creation and Fall: A Theological Exposition of Genesis 1–3*, vol. 1, ed. M. Rüter, I. Tödt, and J. W. de Gruchy, trans. D. S. Bax (Minneapolis: Fortress Press, 2004), 111.

[6] Herbert E. Ryle, *The Book of Genesis in the Revised Version* (Cambridge, UK: Cambridge University Press, 1921), 50.

[7] While Satan is not specifically mentioned in Genesis, Satan is equated with the serpent in Revelation 12:9 and 20:2.

[8] Ryle, *Book of Genesis*, 30–31.

[9] William MacDonald, *Believer's Bible Commentary: Old and New Testaments,* ed. A. Farstad (Nashville: Thomas Nelson, 1995), 36.

[10] Ryle, *Book of Genesis*, 29.

[11] J. D. G. Dunn, "Repentance," in *New Bible Dictionary*, 3rd ed., ed. D. R. W. Wood et al. (Downers Grove, IL: InterVarsity Press, 1996), 1007.

[12] Oswald Chambers, *My Utmost for His Highest* (Grand Rapids, MI: Discovery House Publishers, 2014), June 1 entry.

[13] An in-depth exploration of the temptations Jesus endured, and the principles we can apply to our own lives, can be found in my Bible study *Hagar.*

[14] C. Church, "Fullness of Time," in *Holman Illustrated Bible Dictionary*, ed. C. Brand et al. (Nashville: Holman Bible Publishers, 2003), 605.

[15] W. A. Elwell and B. J. Beitzel, "Messiah," in *Baker Encyclopedia of the Bible*, vol. 2 (Grand Rapids, MI: Baker Book House, 1988), 1446.

[16] R. C. Sproul, *Mark*, 1st ed. (Orlando: Reformation Trust, 2011), 60.

[17] William Barclay, *The New Daily Study Bible: The Gospel of Mark* (Edinburgh: Saint Andrew Press, 2001), 82–83.

[18] Sproul, *Mark*, 60.

[19] Still, Scripture does acknowledge that at times suffering may in fact be a result of a person's own sin. For example, in John 5, Jesus heals another paralytic whom Jesus later warns, "Stop sinning, or something worse may happen to you" (5:14).

NOTES

NOTES

AWAITING GOD'S REIGN

WEEK TWO

Slavery. Disease. Political oppression. Any one of these could easily take first place in today's world headlines. It was no different in Jesus's day. People were suffering and looking for deliverance. And just like today, there was no shortage of people promising solutions. However, there was one affliction no one was able to conquer: *demons*. This week, we journey with Jesus and His disciples as He begins preparing their minds and hearts to enter enemy territory.

"Not everyone who says to me, 'Lord, Lord,' will enter the kingdom of heaven, but the one who does the will of my Father. . . . On that day many will say to me, 'Lord, Lord.' . . . And then will I declare to them, 'I never knew you.'"
—Matthew 7:21–23

DAY ONE
Do You Want to Get Well?

I was thirty years old when I became a Christian. If I had to list my sins up to that point, the scroll would have been miles long. Before graduating high school, I had already broken God's commands "Do not commit adultery" (I had sex outside of marriage) and "Do not murder" (I had an abortion). Before I met Jesus, my pile of sin was so filthy that, looking back, I "did not know how to blush" (Jer. 8:12). But that was all in my past . . . *or so I thought.*

I'll never forget the day. I was still very young in my Christian walk—and I had no idea how vulnerable I was. I found myself in yet another vile pit of sin. It seems the enemy was determined to destroy my testimony before I ever had a chance to share it. For months, it felt as if I were trapped in quicksand. Again and again, I confessed my sin to God, but the harder I struggled, the further I sank.

One day, I finally reached the end of myself. Falling on my face in sorrow and grief, I cried out to God for deliverance. When at last my tears were spent, I looked up. Some would say I saw a vision. I believe Jesus or His angel visited me. I still remember it as if it were yesterday. He wore a simple white robe. I can still picture the glimpse of gold and purple, perhaps a sash or belt, but all too quickly I shut my eyes. *Could this be real?* He then spoke to my spirit. It was not an audible voice, but I'll never forget what I heard. Just three little words: "It is finished."

And it was. Jesus set me free that day, and I've never once gone back to that pit. Although I had previously prayed to receive Jesus as my Savior, I believe that was the day when I truly embraced Him as Lord.

"He drew me up from the pit of destruction . . . and set my feet upon a rock. . . . He put a new song in my mouth, a song of praise to our God." —Psalm 40:2–3

Pause to Ponder

What does it mean that Jesus is *both* Lord and Savior?

What does it mean to you personally?

Read Psalm 40:2–3 and 40:11–12. (Optional: read all of Psalm 40.) In what ways can you relate to the psalmist?

Do You Want to Get Well?

When God allowed me a glimpse into the depth of wickedness I was capable of, it was then that I realized how desperately I needed deliverance, not only from my sin, *but also from myself.*

"Do you want to get well?" Jesus asks. This question is at the heart of today's lesson. The story is found only in the Gospel of John. Chronologically, the story would appear just prior to Mark 3, right around the same time as the events we have been studying.

Read John 5:1–6. What motivation may have been behind Jesus's question?

Pause to Ponder

Imagine Jesus came to you with a similar question. What would the "get well" be for you? How would you fill in the blank: "Do you want ______________________________?"

"For the word of God is living and active, sharper than any two-edged sword, piercing to the division of soul and of spirit . . . and discerning the thoughts and intentions of the heart."

—Hebrews 4:12

Perhaps your "get well" is to heal your marriage or a relationship with a child or parent. Maybe you would ask to be freed from an addiction or habitual sin. Perhaps you hope Jesus will take away a physical illness or even a spiritual one, such as pride or greed. If Jesus came to you and asked if you wanted to be freed from your difficulty, I imagine you would immediately answer yes, but that is not what happens in this story.

Read John 5:7–13; then, answer the questions that follow on this page.

How did the man respond to Jesus's question?

In Jesus's day, "popular belief [held] that the first person into the pool after the waters had been disturbed, and only the first person, would be miraculously healed."[1]

What might the man's response to Jesus's question reveal about his:

Faith/relationship with God?

Outlook on life?

In what ways can you sympathize with the man?

Receiving the Miracle

Let's be honest. Sometimes it is hard to look past our circumstances—especially if our burdens have been weighing heavy for many years. Picture the scene: the

Even when a miracle arrives, we sometimes still cannot see past our circumstances.

man in our story has been crippled for thirty-eight years, but when his miracle arrives, he still cannot see past his circumstances. Instead of embracing the hope Jesus brings, he seems to blame others for his difficulties. Undeterred, Jesus commands him, "Stand up! Pick up your mat and walk," and immediately he is healed.

I do not know about you, but here is where I would expect the man to begin jumping up and down, praising God and thanking Jesus. However, that is not what happens. When the man is rebuked for carrying his mat on the Sabbath, he deflects the accusations, saying, "The man who made me well said to me, 'Pick up your mat and walk.'" Indifferent to the fact that the man had been miraculously healed, his accusers demand to know who told him to violate their sacred laws.[2] The man had no idea; he had never even bothered to ask Jesus His name.

Read John 5:14–15; then, answer the questions that follow.

Who went looking for whom?

How does this speak to your heart personally?

What is Jesus's warning and how does the man respond?

What conclusions can you draw?

Rejecting the Miracle-Giver

"See, you are well! Sin no more, that nothing worse may happen to you."[3] What could be worse than being crippled for thirty-eight years? *A lot*, as it turns out. I don't know about you, but it is at this point that I would expect the man to repent of his sins and follow Jesus. After all, he failed to follow the first time, but now he is given a second chance. Sadly, nothing has changed. Instead of taking Jesus's warning to heart, the man "went away" (on his new legs, mind you!), right back to his accusers to inform them that it was Jesus who healed him. It is as if he is pointing the finger toward Jesus, saying, "That's the man! He is the guilty one, not me!"

He had received the miracle, but he missed the Miracle-Giver.

How sad! Other than the man's physical condition, nothing had changed. He had received the miracle, but he missed the Miracle-Giver. Instead of using his new legs to follow, serve, and dedicate his life to Jesus, he chose to continue walking in darkness, turning a blind eye to his own sins while ever on the lookout for someone to blame.

Lord of the Sabbath

Read John 5:16–18. Why was Jesus being persecuted, and how did He respond?

"He is before all things, and in him all things hold together." —Colossians 1:17

Read Colossians 1:17 in the margin and Hebrews 1:3 in your Bible. How do these verses shed light on Jesus's words in John 5:17?

This last passage conveys a great deal in just a few sentences. In John 5:16, we read that Jesus "was doing these things" on the Sabbath. In Greek, the verb "doing" is active-imperfect, which means that this was a continuous, habitual activity, suggesting that Jesus chose the Sabbath day intentionally.

Then in verse 18, we read that Jesus was "breaking" the Sabbath. The root word for break is *elye* in Greek. It literally means to release, loosen, or unbind. When we consider all that Jesus was doing—releasing people from sickness, unbinding people from demons—just imagine all the people who found *rest* because Jesus was willing to *break* the Sabbath!

Imagine all the people who found *rest* because Jesus was willing to *break* the Sabbath!

Read Mark 2:27–28 and John 5:17. What does it mean that Jesus is "lord of the Sabbath"?

What difference does it make that Jesus has the authority to redefine the Sabbath (or any other religious practice)?

Throughout our lives, you and I will face many trials—even suffering. Some may be due to sin (either ours or others'), but others are simply the fallout of living in a broken world. There may be times when Jesus chooses to step in and rescue us from our circumstances: to grant us temporary *rest* from our suffering. But Jesus would not rest from *His* work until He fulfilled His mission: to rescue our souls. His mercy in this life points us to an even greater rest to come.

Jesus may choose to rescue us from our circumstances, but His greatest mission is to rescue our souls.

Your Turn

Consider the "get well" situation you described on page 55. (If you did not complete that exercise, go back and do it now.) Have you been tempted to blame someone for your circumstances, such as yourself, someone else, or even God? If so, how?

What would it look like to give Jesus "lordship" in this situation?

Perhaps God is using the situation to draw you closer to Him, to teach you some aspect of His character—or yours. Maybe He wants to soften your heart toward another person. Bring the situation to God in prayer. Share what He reveals to you below.

DAY TWO
Facing the Opposition

In Week One, I shared with you how I enjoy setting aside one day with the Lord each week. I call it my "date with Jesus." Because I love the ocean and do not live far from it, I often spend the day at a nearby beach. I'll never forget one day at the beach several years ago. A huge flock of pelicans had flown close to the shore to feed. It is always a treat to see God's magnificent creatures in action. For quite some time, I watched as again and again the pelicans dove into the water. To my surprise, they often came up empty or with just a tiny fish.

Meanwhile, I noticed a small duck about a third of the size of a pelican wading leisurely on top of the water as the pelicans were diving all around him. All of a sudden, the duck dove down into the water. Moments later, it came up with—I kid you not—a fish in its bill that was nearly half its size! For several minutes, I watched the little duck trying to hold on to the huge fish thrashing in its bill. With my brows pinched and my teeth clenched, I didn't think I would rest until the matter was resolved one way or the other. I wasn't even sure if I was cheering for the duck or the fish.

It did take some effort, but eventually that little duck managed to swallow the whole thing. My eyes wide, I imagined he would not eat again for a week. Just then, a giant pelican popped up from underneath the water—bill empty. I suppose I should have felt sorry for the pelican, but I couldn't help but laugh. If he only knew that little duck had just swallowed his prize.

Taking Home the Prize

Perhaps it was the duck's speed or proximity that gave it the advantage. Maybe the large fish just happened to bump the duck's feet in its effort to escape the pelican. The reality is that God cares for all His creatures; but like the two hungry birds I saw that day at the beach, only one took home the prize.

When it comes to God fulfilling the deepest needs of human beings, however, the outcome is never dependent on our ability, or circumstances, or even plain luck. Rather, it is always a matter of the heart. Yesterday, we explored the story of the paralytic in John's Gospel. This story is in stark contrast to the story we read earlier in Mark of another paralytic. Both men were healed, but only one took home the *real prize.*

> When it comes to God fulfilling our deepest needs, the outcome is never dependent on our abilities or our circumstances; rather, it is always a matter of the heart.

Glance back at the story in Mark 2:1-12. Compare these events to the story in John 5. What contrasts can you discover?

I often marvel at the four friends in Mark 2. Life could not have been easy for them—or the paralyzed man—especially in those days when daily living was hard even for the average person. Yet when faced with great obstacles, they refused to give up. They were committed to finding relief for their friend no matter what.

The man in John's Gospel, however, was alone. It could not be his physical condition that stood in the way of him enjoying meaningful relationships (the fact that the other paralytic had friends disproves that theory). I wonder how many times someone attempted to befriend him over the years, only to be driven away by the man's self-pity and pointing the blame at others. While both men suffered from paralysis, this, as far as we can tell, is where the similarities between the two end. One had friends; the other did not. One had faith; the other did not. One gave glory to God; the other did not. One was forgiven, then healed; the other was healed, *then warned.*

Consider again the contrasts between the men in Mark 2 and John 5. How might faith, forgiveness, and giving glory to God be related?

What about unbelief, unrepentance, and unforgiveness?

Both men were in need of God's mercy, and although both were healed, only one walked away in freedom. Here we see that even if a miracle does arrive, people do not always respond in ways we expect.

During New Testament times, the Pharisees, meaning "separate ones," were considered the largest and most influential religious-political party.[4]

Pause to Ponder

Imagine a person prone to self-pity and blaming others. Describe this person's heart.

What might happen if this person stays on that path?

Religious Opposition

At the end of last week's lesson, we saw the first hints of opposition to Jesus. The Pharisees were one of several religious sects in Jesus's day. They controlled the synagogues and wielded significant societal and political influence. As developers of the oral traditions, the Pharisees seemed to have transformed Judaism from a religion of sacrifice to one of law—both written and oral.[5] In effect, they shifted the focus away from God's holiness and mercy onto human behavior. Despite the fact that many were hypocritical, self-righteous, and greedy (see Jesus's harsh assessment in Matthew 23:15, 23–28), they were nonetheless popular and revered by the people. In contrast, the religious elite often looked down upon the common class, who were mostly poor and uneducated.

Read Mark 3:13–15. What responsibility and accompanying authority did Jesus delegate to his twelve apostles?

What reason might Jesus have had for delegating this specific authority?

It is interesting that although Jesus delegates this authority at this point in time, the disciples weren't sent out to exercise it until a few months later (Mark 6:7–12). Apparently, they still had much to learn. In fact, Jesus hinted at this earlier in a brief, yet profound, parable.

Skip back one chapter and read Mark 2:22. Write the last sentence of the verse in the space below.

Whether you have heard teaching on this Scripture or not, what might Jesus be trying to illustrate in this statement? (Hint: read Mark 2:15, 16, 18, and 24.)

While Jesus was ready to fill His disciples with "new wine," the truth is that they were not yet ready to receive it—they were still living in "old wineskins." These *skins* could include religious legalism, hardness of heart, or anything else that hindered them from abandoning all else to follow Jesus. Only when they reached the point of becoming devoted followers would they be ready to preach the good news of His kingdom and exercise authority over demons as His faithful witnesses.

As we discovered last week, during Jesus's earthly ministry, preaching the news of the arrival of the kingdom of God is strongly linked with casting out demons. Having authority over demons in the spiritual realm serves to validate the message that Jesus brings into the earthly realm. When Jesus delegates the responsibility of preaching the kingdom of God to His twelve apostles, He also bestows on them the authority of casting out demons. This is in order to demonstrate the truth of their message.

On a side note: in the excellent and easy-to-read book *What the Bible Teaches about Spiritual Warfare*, authors Robert Dean Jr. and Thomas Ice offer a word of caution for believers today:

> Once the foundation of the church had been laid by the apostles (Eph. 2:20) and the boundary and nature of the gospel message was established, the norm for dealing with demon-possessed unbelievers had become *the preaching of the gospel*. . . . Today, God still performs miracles and frees people from demons, but He performs these actions *directly* rather than indirectly through His people. (Of course, He may do it in response to prayer . . . .)[6]

Read Mark 1:16–20. Compare and contrast these fishermen-turned-apostles with the religious leaders. List as many differences as you can think of.

The New Testament word "apostle," commonly understood as "messenger," literally means "sent one."

Mark 3 is filled with contrasts, and it highlights the increasing hostility against Jesus, especially from those in authority. As we studied last week, after the religious leaders failed to trap Jesus, they joined forces with those having political power in order to plot Jesus's death—not His arrest, not His trial—but His *death*. Wow! And this outright hatred occurs when there is still a year and a half of Jesus's ministry yet to unfold!

However, Jesus then turns the idea of religious authority on its head by delegating *His divine authority* to preach and cast out demons not to the religious elite, but to uneducated fishermen, tax collectors, and other unlikely candidates the Pharisees looked down upon (see Acts 4:13 and Mark 2:14).

"For all authority comes from God, and those in positions of authority have been placed there by God."
—Romans 13:1b NLT

Pause to Ponder

Think of a time when you witnessed someone you deemed an "unlikely candidate" move into a higher position, perhaps a job promotion, leadership position at church, or maybe even as an elected official. Describe the situation and how it made you feel.

How might personal pride or prejudices have affected your reaction?

How might God have used (or be using) the situation for His own purposes?

Legal Opposition

The word "scribe" in Greek is *grammateus*, from the verb *grapho*, meaning "to write." When used in the Gospels, the word "scribe" (also called "lawyers" or "teachers of the law") refers to a class of scholars who copy, teach, and interpret the Jewish law for the people. Many Pharisees arose out of this highly skilled profession.[7]

Read Mark 3:20–27. What accusations are made against Jesus by

His family:

The scribes:

What motivations may have been behind each group's accusations? List as many as you can think of.

Just as the Pharisees recognized that Jesus had the power to work miracles (Mark 3:1–6), the scribes (who traveled roughly one hundred miles to investigate) likewise did not question whether Jesus had the power to cast out demons. The evidence was plain to everyone. Rather, the issue they wrestled with was *by what power* Jesus was able to do these things.

Both the Pharisees and scribes had much to lose. Jesus's popularity, along with His simultaneous display of divine power and apparent disregard for their religious practices, posed a real threat. (Very often, these religious practices stemmed not from Old Testament law, but from oral traditions passed down through generations.) With the crowds flocking to Jesus, these religious leaders were at risk of losing their long-standing and coveted positions of authority and respect.

When they failed to recognize God at work in Jesus, the scribes concluded that Jesus must be an instrument of Satan. Wow! That's quite an accusation! One commentary author writes, "It made no sense to them that God would empower an uneducated carpenter to do such things, especially since He seemed to have so little regard for their [sacred] traditions."[8] Even Jesus's own family did not recognize who Jesus really was. Instead, they set out to stop Him, accusing Him of insanity.

Compare and contrast the scribes' accusations with how the demons referred to Jesus (Mark 1:24, 3:11).

What conclusions can you draw?

No one can encounter Jesus and remain unchanged; we either want to touch Him or trap Him; our hearts are either melted or hardened.

The reactions of the demons reveal that it is possible to know the truth about Jesus and still be deeply hostile toward God. As a matter of fact, no one who came into contact with Jesus exhibited indifference. Their hearts either melted or hardened; they sought to touch Him or trap Him—no one who encountered Jesus left His presence unchanged. Even more, their reactions were often not at all what others might have expected from them. Instead of exalting Jesus, the religious denounced Him; instead of embracing Him, His family denied Him.

Your Turn

In what ways have you experienced being misunderstood, accused of falsehood, or even mistreated by others because of your faith?

People do not always respond to the Good News as we might expect. What implications does this have for you in regard to sharing the gospel?

Whom are you struggling to share your faith with? Spend some time in prayer; ask God for wisdom in how you can minister to these people. Is there a need you can meet? Do you need to forgive them or ask forgiveness? Could there be a spiritual battle? Write down what God reveals to you.

Day Three
Expect the Unexpected

The theme in the classic novel *Lord of the Flies* is a fitting parallel for today's lesson.[9] In the book, a group of boys is stranded on a remote island paradise. With no adults to provide authority and guidance, the boys attempt to govern themselves. It's a disaster. Any gains of order and civility are soon lost to power struggles and the irresistible delights of their newfound freedoms. In time, the boys descend into savagery and even murder before a remnant is rescued in the end.

It's a dramatic story, written by a gifted author who was awarded the Nobel Prize in Literature for his work. Curiously, the title of the book is taken directly from a story found in the Old Testament. The book of 2 Kings begins with Ahaziah, the king of Israel, falling from his upper room and becoming injured. Rather than consulting the living God regarding his fate, he sends messengers to inquire of *Baal-zebub*, the god of Ekron. But God intercepts the king's messengers by sending the prophet Elijah, who challenges the king with God's own message: "Is it because there is no God in Israel that you are going to inquire of Baal-zebub, the god of Ekron?" (2 Kings 1:2–3).

The Hebrew word translated *Baal-zebub* (meaning *lord of flies*) "was a god worshiped by the Philistines at Ekron (2 Kings 1:2–16). . . . During the Second Temple period, when numerous names were used to designate the leader of the forces of evil, one of the names selected was Baal-zebub."[10] In time, the name became synonymous with the designation "prince of demons," which Jesus would simply identify as Satan.

Read 2 Kings 1:2-8 and reread Mark 1:2-6. What similarities can you discover between Elijah and John the Baptist?

Elijah was a famous prophet in Israel; his name means "Yah[weh] is God."

There is only one time in all of Scripture when we are given specific details about Elijah's clothing. That event is when the king of Israel rejects God and turns instead to Baal-zebub, god of Ekron. Elijah is then sent by God to deliver a message. He is described as wearing "a garment of hair, with a belt of leather." It is no coincidence that Scripture includes this identical detail when God sends another messenger, John the Baptist, some nine hundred years later (Mark 1:6). The mention of clothing is an underlying concept in Mark's Gospel. Nothing in Scripture is random. No sooner does John the Baptist begin calling the people to turn back to God, preaching that the kingdom of God is near (Matt. 3:2), than Jesus, the true King, is accused of being possessed by Beelzebul (the Greek equivalent of *Baal-zebub*).

Blasphemy against the Holy Spirit

Reread Mark 3:22-27. Who is the strong man in this parable? (Hint: consider the context. Who is "coming to an end"?)

Read Matthew 12:43-45. What is the house in this illustration?

What might the strong man's house (and goods) in Mark 3:27 represent? (Hint: What does Satan seek to possess? See also Luke 4:5-6.)

What principles can you glean from the illustration in Mark 3:23-27?

In Matthew 12, even after the demon departed, the man had not been changed. Rather, the demon returned to find *his* house "empty, swept and put in order."

Demons are opportunists (Eph. 4:27). Whatever attracted the demon to this man in the first place had not changed.

In Mark 3, we see this reality at work on a larger scale. Satan's "house" represents his dominion, which is earth—humanity's habitation. This is the very dominion our ancestors Adam and Eve forfeited that fateful day in the Garden when they rejected God's authority and were led astray by their own desires (James 1:14). But just as God promised in Genesis 3:15, Jesus here foreshadows the end of Satan's reign. Satan may be the "strong man," but Jesus is the Son of God—*God Almighty*—who alone has the power to "bind the strong man" and "plunder his house."

Pause to Ponder

What does it mean that Jesus can plunder the *strong man's* house? What does this mean to you personally?

Then we reach verse 28. There is perhaps no other passage in the New Testament that has caused more confusion and unnecessary anguish than Mark 3:28–30.

Read Mark 3:28–30.

What do you suppose the "unforgivable sin" might be referring to? List as many possibilities as you can think of.

SUPPLEMENTAL READING

What Is the "Unforgivable Sin"?

All sin breaks God's heart and injures our communion with Him. Yet to the truly repentant, no sin is unforgivable. To better understand the "unforgivable sin" as taught by Jesus, it is important to examine the context. The events recorded in Mark include three key points. The sin was committed:

- By a specific group of people (teachers of the law).
- At a specific time (while Jesus lived on the earth).
- In a specific context (Jesus delivers a man possessed by a demon).

While biblical scholars hold varying opinions concerning the application of this passage, most, if not all, agree that the tragedy lies in the fact that although the scribes acknowledged the miracle, they gave credit to Satan rather than giving glory to God.

As teachers of the law, the scribes not only knew the Scriptures, but they were also responsible for teaching God's law to the people, which held them to a higher accountability before God (James 3:1). Nevertheless, their hearts were so hardened that they not only refused to acknowledge the work of the Holy Spirit performed right in their midst, but they publicly denounced it as the activity of Satan.

In the Old Testament, blasphemy was to speak evil of God (including His works) and was punishable by death. In the context of Mark 3, the blasphemy Jesus denounces as unforgivable is the religious leaders' willful, determined opposition to God and the Holy Spirit. This opposition brings them to the point that nothing can lead them to repentance, since the very power being rejected holds their only hope![11] In effect, they've committed an eternal sin. It is quite sobering to think that Jesus can save a man possessed by demons, but not a man whose heart is completely hardened against the Holy Spirit.

While blasphemy against God (or His Holy Spirit) has plagued human history even up to this day, the issue of the "unforgivable sin" only occurs in the Bible in the specific context of Jesus Himself casting out demons in full view of the people while He was physically on the earth ministering amongst the Jewish people. Jesus confronted the scribes face-to-face. His miracles were witnessed firsthand. Israel was anticipating the appearance of her Messiah (as predicted by the prophet Daniel; see Daniel 9). These conditions were only present in that one specific period of time. Nowhere else in the Bible is the "unforgivable sin" mentioned except in this context (see parallel account in Matt. 12:22–32).

Nevertheless, we dare not misunderstand this to imply that people are not at risk of entering hell today, for this would go against everything Jesus (and the Bible as a whole) taught. Through the cross, all sins are forgivable, but not everyone will choose to embrace God's forgiveness. Today, the risk of hell results from the rejection of the salvation God offers through His Son Jesus (we will explore this more in Week Five).

All sins are forgivable, but not everyone will choose to embrace God's forgiveness.

In contrast, Scripture assures us that all believers—those who have acknowledged and repented of the evil in their hearts and lives and turned to Jesus as their Lord and Savior—have been filled with the Holy Spirit (1 Cor. 3:16; 2 Tim. 1:14). Therefore, they are incapable of blaspheming against the Holy Spirit living within them and never need worry that they've committed the "unforgivable sin."

The war for human souls is real.

The war for human souls is real. Jesus Himself points out that for Satan to battle his own forces would be self-defeating. However, because Jesus exhibits absolute authority over demons, Jesus's work thereby signals the impending demise of Satan's reign altogether. But it signals even more than that. The end of one reign means the beginning of another. Jesus's authority over demons is evidence that the new reign has come—that the powers of darkness, sin, death, and Satan are "coming to an end."

The reality is that the demon-possessed were in great torment. Jesus Christ (*Christos*, meaning "king") came and delivered them, bearing witness to His pronouncement at the start of His ministry: "The time is fulfilled, and the kingdom of God is at hand; repent and believe in the gospel." But not all will embrace His mission.

On the Outside Looking In

The moment Jesus sets foot on the earth, the reality of Satan's doom sends the demons into a panic—as well it should. Yesterday, we witnessed the start of various forms of opposition to Jesus. Being misunderstood, accused of falsehood, or even mistreated by others is painful for any of us, but when the persons are members of our own family, the hurt is far more personal. The Pharisees sought to put Jesus to death; the scribes accused Him of conspiring with Satan. In Mark 3:21, we read that some of Jesus's own family went out to take custody of Him, assuming He had lost His mind. It seems every way He turned, opposition was waiting.

Read Mark 3:31–35; then, answer the questions that follow.

Describe the events in your own words.

Compare Jesus's mother and brothers to the crowd around Him. What contrasts can you discover?

How does Jesus redefine family in this passage?

Do you find Jesus's redefinition of family difficult? Encouraging? Share your thoughts.

In Mark 3:21, we read that several family members sought to take Jesus by force. Mark then specifically identifies Jesus's mother and brothers arriving on the scene a few verses later. Perhaps His mother and brothers were hoping they could reason with Him. One way or another, it now gets personal.

Pause to Ponder

> Imagine you are Jesus's mother. No one knew more than she did that Jesus had come from God. What might be going through your mind if you were in her sandals?
>
> What might she have hoped to gain and at what potential cost?

It would have been reprehensible in those times to leave your own family—especially your own mother—standing outside when they had called for you. Even the most uninformed Jewish child would at least have been familiar with the Ten Commandments, including "honor your father and mother" (Exod. 20:12).

Nevertheless, Jesus rejects His mother and brothers' request to speak with Him. Not only that, but in one swift pronouncement, He uses the event to altogether redefine what "family" means for those who would follow Him. From now on, family is made up of those who come *inside* and sit humbly at Jesus's feet. But Jesus goes even further than that. By adding "sister" to the mix, He has just redefined "disciple" to include both men and women—a radical move in Jesus's day.

Skip ahead for a moment and read Mark 4:11-12. Compare and contrast those who are "inside" with those who are "outside." Who are they? What is at stake? What else can you discover?

In a very short time, Jesus's activities send demons fleeing, Pharisees conspiring, and lawyers blaspheming, and now even His own mother and brothers do not seem to understand Him (at this point). If they had, we would expect them to have asked to come in and listen; surely the crowd would have made room for Jesus's own mother. Instead of seeking to come inside, however, they send a message to Jesus asking Him to come out. In effect, they are asking Him to stop His teaching—to stop what He is doing—*to stop His mission.*

Jesus's words may appear harsh, but He is drawing a stark contrast for the people. Scanning the faces of those seated around Him, Jesus testifies, "Here are my mother and my brothers! *For whoever does the will of God*, he is my brother and sister and mother" (Mark 3:34–35; emphasis mine). Jesus's words imply that, at least at that moment, His mother and brothers were *not* in the will of God. If His family's aim was to cease, slow, or in any way interfere with Jesus's mission—if even for just a moment—then Jesus's assessment is correct.

"For whoever does the will of God, he is my brother and sister and mother."
—Mark 3:35

Your Turn

Are there friends or loved ones "standing outside" the family of God who may be hindering your walk with God? Take a few moments to ask God how you can pray for them. Write a prayer as God leads you.

Day Four

Surveying the Land

Sometimes it can be tempting to skip over passages in Scripture—especially those that have become familiar. Perhaps you have read or heard many sermons regarding the parables Jesus teaches in Mark 4. However, nothing in Scripture is random. There's a reason these parables are placed immediately before Jesus's encounter with Legion, which will become clearer as we move forward. While we are not going to examine all of the parables, we will explore the first one, which begins with Jesus's emphatic command, "Listen!"

The Parable of the Sower

Read Mark 4:1–20. Jesus presents four illustrations; describe the first one along with Jesus's explanation.

How is a person like a *path* in this illustration? What might this mean?

The first Bible verse I ever memorized was Psalm 126:6. To this day, it is a promise I cling to often. In my early years as a Christian, I shared my faith wherever I went and with whomever I came in contact: friends, family, coworkers. . . . Looking back, I feel sorry for anyone ever seated next to me on an airplane. However, it didn't take very long for me to realize that to press onward "carrying seed to sow" often meant I would "go out weeping." I would go out with a heavy heart, knowing that few, if any, would respond to the good news I longed to share.

"Those who go out weeping, carrying seed to sow, will return with songs of joy, carrying sheaves with them." —Psalm 126:6 NIV

Pause to Ponder

Read Psalm 126:6 in the margin. How have you seen this truth exhibited in your own life?

By teaching the parable of the sower, Jesus is preparing His disciples by illustrating the various responses they can anticipate when sharing the gospel. Having already witnessed the varied and volatile responses to Jesus firsthand, His followers are now better able to absorb these sobering truths. Sadly, of the four illustrations, the first three are not very encouraging.

Complete the following chart by describing the first three illustrations as they are represented in the text. (We will discuss the fourth and final illustration later.) In the second column, restate each one in your own words. For the last column, imagine you wanted to warn someone against these dangers. What would you say? I completed the first one to get you started.

Illustration	How would I describe it?	How would I warn others?
The path represents those who hear the Word of God, but Satan quickly takes it away.	*Like a path that hardens over time, these are people whose hearts have hardened; though they hear, they do not accept God's voice.*	*If you hold on to anger, bitterness, self-righteousness, or anything else that pulls you away from God, one day your heart will become so hard that even if God's words reach your ears, they will never penetrate your heart.*

Next, consider each person or group listed below. For each one, fill in the blank with the illustration you think *best* describes their heart condition at the time the events occur in the text. Then share why you think that is. (Note: this exercise is designed for discussion purposes. As some responses call for speculation, there are no right or wrong answers.)

HARDENED PATH   ROCKY GROUND   AMONG THORNS

Leper (Mark 1:40–45)________________

Why?

Pharisees (Mark 3:1–6) ________________

Why?

Jesus's family (Mark 3:20–21) ________________

Why?

Scribes (Mark 3:22–30) ________________

Why?

"The fruit of the Spirit is love, joy, peace, patience, kindness, goodness, faithfulness, gentleness, self-control."

—Galatians 5:22–23

Bearing Fruit for the Kingdom

In my early years as a Christian, I thought "bearing fruit" only meant gaining converts through sharing the gospel. While my motives were genuine—I sincerely grieved for those who did not know Jesus (I still do)—nevertheless, I still had a lot to learn. While one aspect of bearing fruit most certainly relates to reaping a harvest (John 4:36), even then, the harvest results from a transformed life.

God's heart for each one of us is to develop the fruit on the inside: our relationship with Him. To learn who He is, to grow in His love, and to become "sweetened" by His Holy Spirit, who molds us from the inside into godly image-bearers. Only then are we ready to be pressed and squeezed and poured out for Him.

What must precede "bearing fruit"? Explain. (Hint: reread Mark 4:3–8.)

God's greatest desire is that we become "sweetened" by His Holy Spirit, who molds us from the inside into godly image-bearers.

Compare and contrast someone whose life bears the "fruit of the Spirit" with a life that does not.

Why is bearing such fruit important?

So far in Mark, we have encountered the unexpected. The religious leaders are hell-bent on killing Jesus. Teachers of the law publicly denounce Jesus as being in alliance with Satan. Even Jesus's own family accuses Him of insanity. None respond to Jesus in ways most would have expected. We would expect the religious leaders to celebrate Him, the lawyers to advocate for Him, and Jesus's family to venerate Him. Instead, they all turn on Him. Even those who received mercy from Jesus did not always respond favorably toward Jesus, as we discovered in John 5.

The reality is that all of these people were in slavery and blinded to the truth. Their slavery may have been to legalism, pride, fear, or something else. Others were merely looking to Jesus to solve their immediate problems: to heal the sick or to free their loved ones from demon possession. But while Jesus certainly had compassion to do these things, He came to do so much more.

Glance back at Mark 1:15. What is Jesus's message? What is He calling upon people to do?

In Week One, Day Four, we learned that repentance involves two steps. Complete the following sentence using what you learned. (Hint: see page 38.)

Repentance involves __________ from sin and __________ after God.

Keeping this definition of repentance in mind, how are "repent" and "believe in the gospel" connected?

Pause to Ponder

What impact have repenting and believing in the gospel had in your life?

What impact would you like them to have?

Counting the Cost

Have you ever promised Jesus, "I'll follow You wherever You go"? Jesus never promised that following Him would be easy. In fact, he often said quite the opposite (see Matt. 10:25; Luke 14:33; and John 15:20).

Read Mark 4:35. After the parable of the sower, Jesus teaches even more parables about the kingdom of God. Then, without warning or explanation, He gives orders to cross the lake (the Sea of Galilee). In the Gospel of Matthew, it is right at this point that two brief, but curious, conversations occur.

Read Matthew 8:18-22 and then complete the chart. I filled in the first column to get you started.

Who came to Jesus?	How did the person address Jesus?	What did the person say?	How did Jesus respond?
A scribe			
A disciple			

List one or two things that stood out to you in the text and why.

What message do you think Jesus was trying to convey by His responses?

- the Son of Man has nowhere to lay his head

- leave the dead to bury their own dead

Throughout Mark, we continually read of crowds of people following Jesus. Then in Matthew 8, we witness two direct encounters with Jesus up close and personal. On the surface, the scribe and disciple seem sincere, but Jesus knows their hearts.

The scribe still views Jesus as merely "teacher." A sign of respect, certainly, but this would not be the first time the scribe called someone *teacher*. Jesus was just accused of blasphemy and insanity, and for all intents and purposes rejected by both family and society. This is why Jesus can say He has *nowhere to lay His head*. The scribe's words sound noble, but Jesus paints a vivid picture of what following Jesus would be like—and it likely was not at all what the scribe had envisioned.

For the disciple, it seems he at first embraced the call to follow Jesus. "Lord . . ." But when the call becomes costly, the decision is followed by "let me first." It makes no difference what the "first" is. Jesus is the Son of God; He doesn't fit in second place. Jesus's words are intended to shock His hearers. He is once again making a distinction. God's commands include "honor your mother and your father," but Jesus Himself had to leave His family behind for the sake of the kingdom of God (Mark 3:31–35), and His followers can expect to face similar conflicts.[12]

Jesus is the Son of God; He doesn't fit in second place.

Pause to Ponder

Throughout our Christian walk, God will repeatedly call upon us to step out in faith in one form or another. Think of a time when you responded, "Lord, let me first ___________." Fill in the blank. Whether or not your resistance was temporary, what were the results? What was gained? What was lost? What did you learn?

I wish I could say I never responded "me first," but I would be lying. However, when I look back on times I resisted God's voice, I can only imagine the lost blessings, hurts, fears, and missed opportunities I (and perhaps others) suffered. Now, whenever I am faced with following God's call, whatever it may be, I consider not only the cost of what might happen if I do follow, but also the cost of what might happen if I *don't*. I love the fact that when we do finally follow—even if it comes after a time of resisting—God is faithful to receive us with open arms. "If we are faithless, he remains faithful—for he cannot deny himself" (2 Tim. 2:13).

"If we are faithless, he remains faithful—for he cannot deny himself."

—2 Timothy 2:13

Your Turn

Where in your life right now are you bearing fruit for God's kingdom?

Are there areas where you would like to bear more fruit? Explain.

Is God asking you to take a step of faith in some new way? Perhaps into a new ministry? A mission trip? Or maybe He is inviting you into a place of healing or restoration. What would it look like to follow His call? What would it look like if you *don't*?

Bring your desires to God in prayer; ask Him to show you one or two steps you can take this week. Incorporate these into a prayer of commitment below.

Day Five
Crossing into Enemy Territory

I was twelve years old when my parents divorced. My mother, little brother, and I moved into a rent-controlled apartment in Jamaica Queens, New York, where taking the subway was part of daily life—I even rode the subway to school. One Friday evening, my mother and I planned to visit my aunt, who lived in Queens near the outskirts of Long Island (my brother was staying overnight with a friend). The journey would require several subway changes followed by a long bus ride. My only job was to meet my mom in Manhattan at the Chambers Street subway station after she got off from work. From there, we would travel the rest of the way together.

While I often joke that I have no sense of direction (which is true), subway maps are different. The only skill required is an ability to connect the dots. Literally. Red ones. Green ones. Each dot is assigned a number or letter. Once you know which station you want to reach, all you have to do is connect the dots. For a linear thinker like myself, navigating the subways was rather easy.

Sadly, what my mom did not know was that there were two Chambers Street stations. One was near the World Trade Center, where she would be waiting for me, and the other, far less traveled, served as a gateway to the Brooklyn Bridge. (Several years ago, the station was described as one of the most frightening, forgotten, and neglected subway stations in the entire New York City subway system.)

I was glad I had bought a slice of pizza with my extra change before I left the station in Queens, as it took a long time to arrive at the Chambers Street station where my mother would be waiting (or so I presumed). When I went upstairs and exited the turnstile, I did not find myself in a large station bustling with people and activity as I had expected. Instead, the filthy station was completely deserted. Frightened and alone, I had no money or tokens to get back down to the platform. It was now getting late. Judging by the decrepit state of the station, I didn't dare go up to the street level. The grumpy-looking man behind the bulletproof window of the cashier's booth ignored me. Leaning against a graffiti-covered wall, I began to cry. It seemed like hours passed with no one coming or going.

Then suddenly, I heard laughter. A beautiful, well-dressed Black couple came down the stairs from the street above. Seeing me, they immediately came over and asked what was wrong. I'll never forget the woman's friendly smile or the man's long, tan, wool coat. They paid my fare, and when we reached the platform below, they provided money for me to use the pay phone. I called the apartment, but no one answered. Then I tried calling my aunt, since that was where my mother and I were actually headed that night. I still remember the combination of panic and overwhelming relief in my mother's voice when my aunt handed her the phone. She told me to head back to the apartment, and she would meet me there as soon as she could.

I hung up the phone and returned to the couple waiting nearby. The woman asked where I lived, and when I responded, her face lit up. "What a coincidence; we're going right past there!" We rode the trains all the way back to Jamaica Queens. As we neared my station, the man asked me how far my apartment was. "About ten blocks," I said. He immediately took out his wallet and handed me a ten-dollar bill. Looking straight at me, he made sure I understood his words: "Take the first taxi you see." I don't remember if I said thank you or even goodbye. I never even asked their names.

I exited the station. Once on street level, I saw a taxi parked at the curb. I climbed into the back seat. The elderly driver turned around and smiled just as a cute little dog jumped up to face me, tail and tongue wagging in excitement. I immediately relaxed into the worn, cracked leather. When the driver reached my apartment building, he watched from the curb until I was safely inside.

Pause to Ponder

Describe a time when a stranger
went out of his or her way to help you.

What sacrifices did the stranger
make, and what did you gain?

When I reflect back on the time I was lost in the subway, I shudder to think what the enemy would have done had he been given half a chance. While the enemy would have more opportunities in years to come, for whatever reason, God held his hand back that night—and I am eternally grateful. The sacrifices of the couple may seem small (a few dollars and perhaps an hour's time), but to a lost twelve-year-old girl, I believe they made the difference between life and death. To this very day, I wonder if they were actually angels in disguise. While I'll never know this side of heaven, of one thing I am certain: it was God who sent them that night to bring me safely home.

Uncharted Waters

Read Mark 4:35–36 (verse 35 is review); then, answer the questions that follow.

It is now evening. What had Jesus been doing all day (Mark 4:1–34), and what does He want to do next?

What might Mark be trying to convey by including the small detail "they took him . . . just as he was" in verse 36?

Imagine you are with Jesus. How might you have reacted—if only in your thoughts—to Jesus's plan?

Jesus had spent a full day teaching. It's now getting late. The Sea of Galilee is roughly seven to eight miles wide. It is situated seven hundred feet below sea level and is surrounded by mountains that rise three to four thousand feet above sea level on the west, north, and east.[13] The journey across would take approximately one to two hours by sailboat on a good day, but due to the lake's location where warm tropical air from the lake's surface rises and meets the colder air from the nearby hills, sudden and violent storms are common.[14]

I don't know about you, but I might be tempted to question the wisdom of crossing the lake. First of all, it's getting dark. Everyone is tired. No one planned for this trip; supplies have not been gathered. Besides, what's the big hurry? Oh, and isn't the other side Gentile territory? Why are we crossing the lake anyway?

It would be hard not to wonder what Jesus was thinking. However, Scripture actually does provide us with some indication. While we only examined the first parable in Mark 4, all the parables in that chapter center on the same theme. In Mark 4:11, Jesus tells His disciples plainly, "To you has been given the secret of the kingdom of God." Jesus had just spent all day *teaching* His disciples various principles about the kingdom of God; now He wanted to *show* them.

A Storm Is Brewing

Read Mark 4:37–38. What did the disciples say to Jesus?

What can you infer from their question?

"[He] stills the roaring of the seas, the roaring of their waves, the tumult of the peoples."
—Psalm 65:7

These seasoned sailors would have battled many raging storms on the Sea of Galilee. Being nearly seven hundred feet below sea level and sandwiched between valleys on one side and mountain ranges on the other, the sea is vulnerable to violent windstorms due to colliding warm and cold air. Nevertheless, these experienced fishermen feared for their lives, giving us a dramatic picture of the intensity of this particular storm.

Glance back at Mark 1:17, and then answer the following questions. What promise did Jesus make?

Imagine you are Simon or Andrew. What do you envision becoming a "fisher of men" would be like?

How does your mental image of becoming a "fisher of men" compare to what the disciples have experienced so far?

Jesus never promised that following Him would be easy. Successful fishing often involves weather forecasting for calm waters, charting a course, a strong boat, proper tools and supplies, and a capable crew, to name just a few. Fishing for *people*, however, is going to look quite different. The command to "go" can come at any time, anywhere. You may not have with you what you think you need for the trip. You may be tired. A storm may be brewing. You may be asked to enter "enemy" territory. In short, all human elements involving control and prediction are removed.

Read Mark 4:39–41. What two commands does Jesus speak in verse 39, and what are the results? Be specific.

What might these veteran fishermen have found especially remarkable?

I love the fact that God designed beautiful and poetic order into our natural world. This would also include what we refer to as the physical laws of cause and effect. For these seasoned fishermen, to see Jesus silence the howling wind would be one thing, but to witness the violent churning water becoming instantly calm would be quite another.

Pause to Ponder

Consider Jesus's rebuke in Mark 4:40. How are fear and faith connected?

How about for you? How are fear and faith connected in your life?

The disciples had witnessed Jesus's power over disabilities, disease, and even demons. He now displays His authority over creation itself. Immediately at His Word, the winds cease and the raging waters calm. These fishermen were well acquainted with the Sea of Galilee. They knew all there was to know about fishing, boats, and sailing. After all, they were fishermen. But Jesus wanted to make them into something new. That was going to mean seeing things differently and doing things they had never done before. Perhaps Oswald Chambers said it best when he wrote, “Beware of [looking] back to what you were once when God wants you to be something you have never been.”[15]

Your Turn

How might God be calling *you* to be something you have never been?

What fears might be holding you back? How may God be trying to prepare you to move past these fears?

What is the next step will you take? Write a prayer of commitment below.

Lesson Summary

What Scripture, statement, or thought was most significant to you this week? Write it down and then reword it into a prayer of response to God.

Notes

[1] D. A. Carson, *The Gospel According to John* (Grand Rapids, MI: Wm. B. Eerdmans, 1991), 243.

[2] John’s Gospel simply describes the man’s accusers as “the Jews”; however, John 5:18 reveals that these are the same ones seeking to kill Jesus. Based on Mark 3:1–6, we can infer that John is referring to those in authority.

[3] While Scripture never teaches that all illnesses are due to personal sin (Job; John 9:3), here we see at least one incident where they are in fact tied together. Jesus uses the events to warn the man of "something worse." If we read further, we realize Jesus is referring to eternal judgment (John 5:21, 24).

[4] Clayton Harrop and Charles W. Draper, "Pharisees," in *Holman Illustrated Bible Dictionary*, ed. C. Brand et al. (Nashville: Holman Bible Publishers, 2003), 917.

[5] Harrop and Draper "Pharisees," *Holman Illustrated*, 917.

[6] Robert Dean Jr. and Thomas Ice, *What the Bible Teaches about Spiritual Warfare* (Grand Rapids, MI: Kregel Publications, 2000), 146, 153.

[7] D. J. Wiseman, "Scribe," in *New Bible Dictionary*, 3rd ed., ed. D. R. W. Wood et al. (Downers Grove, IL: InterVarsity Press, 1996), 1068.

[8] R. C. Sproul, *Mark*, 1st ed. (Orlando: Reformation Trust, 2011), 68.

[9] William Golding, *Lord of the Flies* (London: Faber and Faber, 1954).

[10] "The actual name may have been Baal-zebul, meaning 'lord of the lofty abode,' but Israelites who considered this god an unworthy rival to Israel's God corrupted it to the word for 'lord of flies' (Baal-zebub)." J. M. Efird, "Baal-zebub," in *The HarperCollins Bible Dictionary*, 3rd ed., ed. M. A. Powell (New York: HarperCollins, 2011), 74.

[11] "Blasphemy," William Smith, *Smith's Bible Dictionary* (Nashville: Thomas Nelson, 1986).

[12] Ulrich Luz, *Matthew: A Commentary*, ed. H. Koester (Minneapolis: Augsburg, 2001), 19.

[13] "Mark 4:35–37," *Nelson's New Illustrated Bible Commentary*, ed. Earl Radmacher, Ronald B. Allen, and H. Wayne House (Nashville: Thomas Nelson, 1999).

[14] "Galilee, Sea Of," in *Baker Encyclopedia of the Bible,* vol. 1, ed. Walter A. Elwell et al. (Grand Rapids, MI: Baker, 1988), 837.

[15] Oswald Chambers, *My Utmost for His Highest* (Grand Rapids, MI: Oswald Chambers Publications, 1986), June 8 entry.

NOTES

NOTES

PART II

THE BATTLE

NOTES

WEEK THREE

SEEKING GOD'S REFUGE

WE HAVE CERTAINLY COVERED A LOT OF MATERIAL IN THE past two weeks. From the Garden of Eden to the Sea of Galilee, we have witnessed everything from a deceiving serpent to outright demon possession. In the same way that Jesus had been preparing His disciples for what lies ahead, our overview of Genesis 1 through 3 and the beginning of Mark's Gospel have been preparing us as we head into enemy territory.

DAY ONE
A Test of Faith

(Optional: reread Mark 4:35–41.)

Let's do a quick review. Many of the disciples had been traveling with Jesus more than a year[1] when Jesus decides to cross the Sea of Galilee. Historians speculate that the kind of boat they used would have had a large central mast and sail, been roughly twenty-seven feet long and eight feet wide, and had a capacity of about fifteen people.[2]

I want you to imagine that you are one of Jesus's disciples in the boat. No sooner do you set out across the lake than a ferocious storm hits. Thick darkness

races across the sky. Violent winds howl all around you. Suddenly, the ties of the sails rip loose. The winds swell to a deafening roar as the sails whip wildly above your head. Raging waves pummel the boat as the rising water threatens to knock you off your feet—

—and Jesus is at the back of the boat, asleep on a cushion.

Panicking, you shake Jesus awake: *Teacher! Don't you care that we're going to drown?!*

Pause to Ponder

Have you ever wanted to cry out to God, *"Don't you care that . . . ?!"* When God is silent, have you felt like He was being indifferent or punishing you or otherwise insensitive to your needs? Share your thoughts.

It is here where we get our first glimpse into the disciples' hearts: they mistook Jesus's tranquility and trust for apathy.[3] Fortunately for the disciples (and us!), God is patient, and God is kind. Jesus knew His disciples still had much to learn.

"You keep him in perfect peace whose mind is stayed on you, because he trusts in you." —Isaiah 26:3

Read Isaiah 26:3 in the margin. Underline the two phrases that describe what peace is anchored in. Then place a circle around the word the phrases have in common. What conclusions can you draw?

Imagine you are still on the boat in the middle of the storm. Calmly, Jesus rouses from His slumber and instantly quiets the wind and calms the waves. Then, turning to *you*, He says, *Why are you so afraid? Have you still no faith?*

What might you be feeling or thinking in that moment?

If you felt you could speak freely, what would you say?

Consider Jesus's words carefully: "Why are you so afraid?" Do you suppose Jesus was offended? Disappointed? Something else? Share your thoughts.

When Faith Becomes Personal

It is when the disciples realize their very lives are at risk that they come face-to-face with their first true test of faith. Following Jesus *just got personal.* And Jesus appears none too impressed with the disciples' response. Did you notice that Jesus was not offended that His disciples were afraid, but rather that they were *so afraid.*[4] It seems that their fear had crossed a line. Let's see if we can put this into perspective.

In the chart, I have outlined in chronological order each miracle in Scripture the disciples[5] witnessed prior to crossing the Sea of Galilee. Using the Scripture references provided, fill in the blanks with a brief description of the miracle. I have completed several for you, including those not mentioned in Mark.

Reference	What miracle(s) did Jesus perform?
John 2:1–11	*Turns water into wine*
John 4:46–54	*Heals a royal official's son*
Luke 5:1–11	*Miraculous catch of fish*
Mark 1:21–28	
Mark 1:29–34	*Heals Peter's mother-in-law (also heals others and casts out demons)*
Mark 1:39	
Mark 1:40–42	
Mark 2:1–12	
John 5:1–9	*Heals an invalid*
Mark 3:1–6	
Mark 3:10–11	*Heals various people with diseases and casts out demons*
Luke 7:1–10	*Heals a centurion's servant*
Luke 7:12–15	*Raises a widow's son from the dead*

Take a few moments to read through the list. Considering all that the disciples have witnessed so far, do you find Jesus's rebuke in Mark 4:40 reasonable? Harsh? Something else? Explain.

For over a year, the disciples have witnessed miracle after miracle after miracle. While they were wise to run to Jesus for help, the magnitude of their fear betrayed their hearts: they believed they were going to drown. In effect, they believed God had abandoned them. But this is not the first time in history that God's people felt this way. To help us gain a better perspective, we will spend the rest of today's lesson briefly exploring three Old Testament stories where God's people feared for their lives and felt abandoned.

A Pagan King versus God's Promises

The scene is ancient Egypt. The Israelites are in slavery when God inflicts the ten famous plagues: blood, hail, locusts, darkness, death . . . miracle after miracle after miracle—all within a span of barely a year.[6] Finally, the king (Pharaoh) of Egypt lets the Israelites go free. Triumphant, God's people head into the wilderness led by Moses.

Read Exodus 14:1-2, 10-11, and 19-22. (Optional: read all of 14:1-22.) List at least three similarities between these events and the events in Mark 4:35-41.

Compare and contrast the Israelites' response in Exodus 14:10-11 with the disciples' in Mark 4:38. What observations can you make?

"Years of rebellion against God have bred in us a fear that cannot be overcome in a day." —A. W. Tozer

These events share some striking similarities. In both stories, the sea poses a real threat. Fearful, the people cry out to the Lord, after which He supernaturally alters the motion of both wind and sea. But underneath all that is happening, we get a glimpse into the hearts of the people—and in both cases, they accuse God of abandoning them to die. The Israelites had more faith in a pagan king than in God's promises. The disciples had more fear of their circumstances than confidence in Jesus's presence.[7] Why? I think A. W. Tozer summed up the human condition well when he wrote, "Years of rebellion against God have bred in us a fear that cannot be overcome in a day"—or even a year, it seems.[8]

Pause to Ponder

As you aim to follow and serve God, do you ever find yourself surprised when things do not go your way? Explain.

Running Away versus Facing Our Fears

The Bible is filled with stories of the miraculous: creation itself, parting the Red Sea, a worldwide flood . . . but perhaps no other story leaves readers scratching their heads more than the story of Jonah. A man survives three days in the belly of a massive fish . . .

Read Jonah 1:1–6. Compare and contrast this passage with Mark 4:35–41. List every similarity and difference you can discover.

As you compared these two passages, what one thing stood out to you the most? Why?

The two stories share some obvious parallels, not the least of which is that both Jonah and Jesus are asleep below deck while a violent storm wreaks havoc overhead. However, it is the blatant contrast in the story that seems so striking. Jonah is running away from his mission, whereas Jesus is heading toward it—yet both are being pummeled by a raging storm. How can this be? To shed light on this question, we will step into our final Old Testament story: the story of Job.

> "[God] commanded and raised the stormy wind, which lifted up the waves of the sea. . . . He made the storm be still, and the waves of the sea were hushed."
>
> —Psalm 107:25, 29

Who Is in Control? God, Nature, or Satan?

If you recall, we briefly explored this story in Week One. Job was a blameless man who feared God. One day, God brags to Satan about Job's faith and godly character. Satan then accuses God of coddling Job, claiming that if Job were robbed of all he had and all he held dear, he "would curse you to your face."

Reread Job 1:12. What authority did God grant Satan, and what parameters did He set?

Read Job 1:13–19. Summarize the events in your own words.

Is there anything in Job 1:13–19 that surprises you? Disturbs you? Share your thoughts.

No one argues that Job suffered immense loss. Satan not only carefully calculated the day on which the destruction would take place (a day of celebrating the eldest son's birthday; see Job 1:4, 18), but he also calculated the methods by which he would inflict suffering on this innocent man and his family. In addition to using invasions by enemy tribes, Satan employed the natural disasters of lightening and violent windstorms.

Concerning the last tragedy, one commentary author explains that it was impossible for Job to avoid bringing God into the picture, since lightning and wind were commonly recognized as God's judgment on the wicked. Of course, that painful picture is precisely what Satan was aiming for. The author then goes on to say, "The other losses were intended to soften him up; this [last] one was [meant] to shatter him."[9] Another writes, "Both wind and lightning . . . were employed by Satan as his tools. God can permit him such control over factors of the weather when it suits the divine purpose, but God retains ultimate control."[10]

The last statement above is key. God is Creator and Sovereign Ruler of the universe. Satan can do nothing without God's permission (Job 1:12). While God may choose to give Satan temporary power over things such as the weather for His own purposes, that is the extent of Satan's power when it comes to natural phenomenon. Ultimately, it all resides within the sovereign will of God.

If Jesus encountered resistance in His mission, we can be sure that we will as well.

Your Turn

Just as God used the wind and sea to stop Jonah from going in the wrong direction, the wind and sea appear to threaten Jesus from going in the *right* direction. Whether this was God's own doing in order to test the disciples' faith or the activity of Satan, Jesus never promised that following Him would be easy. If Jesus encountered resistance in His mission, we can be sure that we will as well.

Ponder those times in your life when you encountered difficult circumstances. Compare the times when you experienced peace with the times you did not. What made the difference?

Glance back at Isaiah 26:3 on page 88 (or in your Bible). Knowing that trials and difficulties lay ahead (John 16:33; 1 Pet. 1:6), what one step will you take this week to fortify your "anchor" of peace? For example, you may want to write Isaiah 26:3 on a note card and commit it to memory. Write your commitment in the form of a prayer below.

> The Gospels of Matthew, Mark, and Luke are referred to as synoptic because, unlike the Gospel of John, they present the life and ministry of Jesus from a similar point of view.

DAY TWO
Stepping onto Enemy Territory

Every once in a while, we come across a passage of Scripture that, on the surface, appears to contradict another passage. In the encounter with Legion beginning in Mark 5, a few curious contradictions in the other Gospel accounts are prone to cause confusion. So we are going to address these before diving further into the story. So sit back, relax, and get ready as we set the stage for Jesus's encounter with Legion.

Which One Do We Believe?

All three writers of the synoptic Gospels (Matthew, Mark, and Luke) were inspired to include the events surrounding the story of Legion. Even Mark, whose Gospel is the shortest, was led by the Holy Spirit to include this specific story. Curiously, Mark is also the one who provides us with the most detail.

(Optional: To get an overview of the story, read all of Mark 5:1–20. You may also want to read the other two accounts in Matthew 8:28–34 and Luke 8:26–39.)

> "God is not man, that he should lie, or a son of man, that he should change his mind." —Numbers 23:19

It is important for you and me to remember that as the Word of God, Scripture can never contradict Scripture. If we find some small detail that appears to conflict with another passage, careful examination will often shed light on the matter. While Matthew, Mark, and Luke all write from a similar perspective, the Holy Spirit inspired each writer to emphasize some details over others, depending upon the audience to which each one was writing. Matthew wrote to a Jewish audience, whereas the Gospels of Mark and Luke were written with Gentile readers in mind.

Read Matthew 8:28, Mark 5:1–2, and Luke 8:26–27.

List the facts that all three narratives share in common.

What aspects of the story are different?

On the surface, it would seem that the only details the Gospel writers agree upon at this point are that the person or persons in the story . . .

- Had a demon (or evil spirit)
- Had come out from the tombs
- Came to Jesus immediately upon Jesus's arrival in the region

"They came to the other side of the sea, to the country of the Gerasenes." —Mark 5:1

Gerasenes or Gadarenes?

Let's address the first discrepancy: Where are they? In the land of the Gerasenes or the Gadarenes? Scholars have proposed a variety of reasonable explanations to account for the discrepancy. The text itself also provides us with some clues.

Look once again at Matthew 8:28, Mark 5:1, and Luke 8:26. How does each author describe the location where Jesus arrives? Be specific.

Matthew:

Mark:

Luke:

Imagine that I lived in your town or city and asked you to describe to me the general vicinity of your home (without using GPS or maps). Now imagine how you would describe it to someone living in another city. How about someone from another part of the country? While all three of your responses would be correct, I suspect that they would nonetheless be different, depending on how familiar the other person was with the area you were describing.

This is likely what is happening here. Did you notice that, while the Gospel writers differ on the name of the area, all three describe the location as being *the country* (or region) *of* either Gerasenes or Gadarenes? This is important. In English, when you and I think of the word "country," we often picture a specific land with a distinct national identity and physical boundaries. However, the word used in Greek is *choran* and is better understood as relating to a general area, district, or region. Scripture also provides another clue. Based on the grammar in the original Greek text, the words *Gerasenes* and *Gadarenes* are not proper nouns in and of themselves, but instead serve as adjectives to describe the country (region) where Jesus arrives.

In other words, rather than pinpointing an exact location, each Gospel writer chose to reference a region that was closest to the general area where the events took place as well as one familiar to his readers. For Matthew's Jewish audience, the region of Gadarenes refers to the area inhabited by residents living in and around Gadara, an important city along the eastern shore of the Sea of Galilee—right across from where Jesus would have set sail. For the Roman and Greek readers of Mark's and Luke's Gospels, the affluent Roman city of Gerasa, situated about thirty-five miles southeast of the Sea of Galilee, would have been more widely known.[11] Also, the name Gerasa was often used to describe the wider geographical area in which the city Gadara was located.[12] Either way, Mark and Luke referenced the region of Gerasenes, as this would be an area their readers would easily recognize.[13]

SUPPLEMENTAL READING

One Demoniac or Two?

Another question that some may find curious is whether there was one man or two. Mark and Luke write about one man, while Matthew mentions two. In fact, throughout his Gospel, Matthew has a habit of pointing out doubles in places where the other authors focus on only one (such as two blind men versus one, Jesus entering Jerusalem on a donkey *and* a colt, and the two demoniacs).[14]

Interestingly, if you were to read the story in Matthew, which totals a mere seven verses (Matt. 8:28–34), and compare it to either Mark or Luke's account, you would find that Matthew also leaves out large segments of the story. Although Matthew witnessed the events firsthand, even the redemptive elements are missing from his story. Matthew simply has a different focus in mind. In contrast, Mark and Luke go into far greater detail. Therefore, it may be that the second man briefly mentioned by Matthew was less known and less prominent in the story, or that the outcome of the second man was simply less noteworthy.

Some scholars leave the issue of one or two demoniacs unresolved. Others view the one demoniac described by Mark and Luke as the primary character in the events, supposing that "two demoniacs would not have associated [with one another], unless the one had been dependent upon the other."[15] For the purposes of this study, given that Mark (and Luke) provides far greater detail of the events and writes about only one demoniac, we will continue our journey in Mark's Gospel and likewise focus our attention on the one man.

Reverent Worship or Resentful Submission?

"When Jesus had stepped out on land, there met him a man from the city who had demons." —Luke 8:27a

Think back on Day Five of last week's lesson, and then answer the following questions. (Hint: glance back at Mark 4:35–41.) During what part of the day did Jesus set sail with His disciples?

Does it seem that anyone besides Jesus anticipated this journey?

Read Luke 8:27a in the margin along with Mark 5:2 and 5:6 in your Bible (we will explore Mark 5:3–5 tomorrow).

How do these verses (along with what you learned in Mark 4:35–41) demonstrate that the demoniac knew Jesus had arrived in the region, even before he actually met Him?

"Oh come, let us worship and bow down; let us kneel before the LORD, our Maker!" —Psalm 95:6

What motivation may have been behind the man bowing down before Jesus in verse 6? List as many possibilities as you can think of.

Most translations[16] of the Bible translate the actions in verse six as "he ran and fell [or bowed or knelt] down before him"; however, a few[17] translate these actions as "he ran and worshiped him." This could be misleading for some. In biblical times (both Old and New Testament), "worship" meant both an acknowledgment of God's worth and glory and a response of praise and adoration. Therefore, in practice, to bow down and to worship were synonymous yet also went hand in hand (see Ps. 95:6 in the margin).

The Greek word in Mark 5:6 is *prosekynesen.* It is where we get the English verb to prostrate oneself. While the word in the New Testament often signifies worship, it can also simply refer to the physical act of bowing down without any heartfelt praise or reverence, such as before a ruler. Scholars differ as to what motivation—and which personality—is behind the man's actions. Perhaps the action reflects the tormented man himself running in desperation to reach and worship Jesus.[18] One commentary author suggests that the behavior is initiated by the demons, yet acknowledges that it is unclear whether it is "counterfeit worship or conniving submission."[19] Maybe both personalities are involved; a possibility vividly captured by another commentary author, who writes, "How true and terrible a picture is this—a man bowed in adoration, petition and faith, and yet hating, defiant and fearing; a double personality, longing for liberty and yet clinging to [rage]."[20] However, Scripture does offer us some clues.

In Mark 4:35–41, we read that Jesus set sail with his disciples in the evening. It also seems that none of the disciples planned for the journey. Not only does Jesus's command to cross the lake appear abruptly, but Scripture also tells us that the disciples took Jesus "just as He was." This suggests that they did not have time to gather supplies or otherwise prepare for the journey. We are told that when they reached the other side, the man came running "from a distance" in order to meet Jesus. Not only that, but both Mark's and Luke's Gospels reveal that the man met Jesus the moment He stepped out of the boat, which means that the man began running toward Jesus even before the boat reached the shore.

"How true and terrible a picture is this . . . a double personality, longing for liberty and yet clinging to [rage]."
—William MacDonald

When we consider that it was getting dark, no messenger could have reached the other side with the news that Jesus was coming. Also, since the man came running from a distance before the boat landed, it seems clear that he knew Jesus had arrived before actually meeting Him. However, on his own, the *human* could have had no way of knowing this. Even seeing Jesus from a distance could not account for this knowledge. After all, this was centuries before photographs: How would people who had never met Jesus know what He looked like? And even if they did have some kind of description, could they really recognize Him from a distance *at dusk?* Only demons, who can see the spirit realm, could have recognized from a distance the Light of the World (John 8:12) invading their territory.

Pause to Ponder

When you consider the spiritual realm, how do you tend to regard it? As separate and distant from the physical world you see? Active and present in your circumstances? Share your thoughts.

Glance back at Mark 3:11, and then answer the questions that follow. Who does Mark attribute the "falling down" to? Circle one.

unclean spirits   possessed persons

Based on what you've learned from Mark's Gospel up to this point, does it seem that this particular reaction of the unclean spirits occurs only occasionally? Explain.

How do these truths shed light on Mark 5:6?

All Jesus did was set foot in the region, and the resident demoniac immediately charged toward Him. Mark tells us that whenever the demons saw Jesus, they fell down before Him. Although the people, including Jesus's disciples, did not yet recognize who Jesus was, the demons knew—*and shuddered* (James 2:19).

Your Turn

How can you take comfort in knowing that demons must concede to Jesus's authority over them?

In what specific area of your life does the enemy currently have the upper hand? (Hint: ponder where you may be held captive to fear, anxiety, shame, anger, or bitterness.)

Spend some time in prayer, asking God if something may be hindering you from having victory in this area. Write down what He reveals to you.

Day Three
Facing Your Demons

I was thirty years old the year I asked Jesus to be the Lord of my life. I could never have imagined that barely six months later my husband would file for divorce. Looking back, I now recognize that our relationship was plagued with dysfunction: he was a volatile alcoholic, and I suffered from codependency and depression. After the divorce, I found myself living alone for the first time. The nightmares started almost immediately. Sometimes they even crept into my thoughts during the day, crippling me with fear. I tried everything. First, I attempted to focus on "positive thoughts." When that failed, I began to monitor what I ate before bedtime. I even tried listening to soothing music before going to sleep. Nothing worked.

One Sunday morning at church, I shared my struggle with a friend who had been a Christian for many years. Gently taking my hands into hers, she asked, "Have you asked God to take the nightmares away?" My mouth fell open as I stared at her in disbelief. "You mean, God can take control over what I *dream*?" I asked. I was stunned. It never occurred to me that I could surrender my nightmares to God. Once I did, they stopped. That was over twenty years ago—and, praise God, the nightmares have never returned.

It seems that in my ignorance, I had divided aspects of my life into two categories: those which I believed God had the power to control and those areas where I presumed I was on my own. The enemy is delighted with our ignorance, as it always provides him an advantage. Twenty years ago, I had no idea I could ask God to take away my nightmares. Today, I know better, but that does not mean I do not have other weaknesses that the enemy will stop at nothing to exploit. Wherever we believe God to be powerless, we give the enemy a foothold.

Wherever we believe God to be powerless, we give the enemy a foothold.

Pause to Ponder

Describe a time when you experienced a difficult situation and tried repeatedly to fix the problem yourself. What grief, agony, or frustration might you have avoided if you had first taken the matter to God in prayer?

The Unseen Realm

Today, we live in a world where information is at our fingertips. In an instant, we can find someone to give an explanation for or solution to virtually any problem we face. However, if we are not careful, not only are we in danger of dismissing the reality that God is sovereign over all, but this tendency to default to human problem-solving can lead to blind spots when it comes to spiritual battles. You and I are more than physical, emotional, and intellectual beings—we are also spiritual beings who live within an unseen, but very real, spiritual realm.

Our tendency to default to human problem-solving can lead to blind spots when it comes to spiritual battles.

Read Mark 5:3. Where was the man living?

Reread Matthew 12:43–45, which we briefly explored last week. What are unclean spirits searching for?

In light of Mark 5:3 and Matthew 12:43–45, what did the unclean spirits gain, and what did the man lose?

Describe one or two general principles you can glean from these truths.

Whenever the enemy gains the upper hand in our lives, we will always suffer loss. It may be loss of reputation, possessions, relationships, or something else.

Pause to Ponder

Think back on a time when the enemy tried to gain the upper hand in your life. What did he stand to gain, and what did you stand to lose?

I'll never forget one summer night when I was twelve years old. I was living with my mother and younger brother in an apartment building in Queens, New York, that stood just a few blocks from an old graveyard. One evening, a group of friends and I were sitting along the curb talking. Just as it was getting dark, a neighborhood boy came along and dared us to walk (or run!) through the graveyard.

My friends and I glanced at one another, the apprehension evident on our faces; however, not wanting to turn down a dare, we accepted the challenge. As our little band of gangly twelve-year-olds began walking through the cemetery, it did not take long before someone got spooked. Within minutes, fear swept over us like a ghostly wail as we took off screaming toward the entrance as fast as our spindly legs could carry us.

Read John 8:44. Why might a burial place for the dead be attractive to the devil and his demons?

For the man in Mark 5, the demons could have compelled him to live in any number of places. They could have chosen a pagan temple or brothel or some other place where evil reigned; but instead, they chose to live among the tombs. Along the lake's edge would have been many caves carved out of the limestone, and many of these caves were used as burial tombs for the dead.[21] But there may be even more going on here than meets the eye. Ancestor worship was common among the surrounding pagan regions. Rituals included praying to the deceased and offering food, wine, and in some cases even blood. Sacrifices were common, not only as gifts to the deceased but also as celebratory meals for the family.[22]

When we consider that Scripture describes the devil as a murderer and liar (John 8:44), it should not be so surprising that Satan and his demons operate and reside in the realm of death and sacrilegious pagan worship. In fact, an abode of the dead seems a fitting home.

The Enemy's Chains

Read Mark 5:3–5 and Luke 8:27 and 29, then answer the questions that follow.

Record all the ways this man was suffering according to the text.

Try to imagine what this man's life was like. In what other ways would he have been suffering? List as many as you can think of.

From the list you just made, which do you personally feel is most tragic? Why?

The suffering of this man seems almost surreal. Surrounded by death and tormented by demons, he was bound again and again only to break the iron chains and shackles and run screaming into the night. Homeless, friendless, outcast, naked, tormented of mind, body, and soul; he was still alive, yet living among the dead. . . .

In addition to chaining his wrists and shackling his feet, how else did the townspeople try to control the man? (Hint: glance back at Luke 8:29.)

Picture yourself being a resident of that town. How might you have responded? Would you agree that it was best to keep the man bound? Explain.

Now imagine being one of the guards. Would you answer the previous question any differently? Why or why not?

The Temple of the Holy Spirit

"For he who is in you is greater than he who is in the world." —1 John 4:4b

Unlike angels, demons cannot make themselves visible. Rather, they need another entity to work through when they want to manifest their presence.[23] This explains why the demons sought to inhabit the poor man. Still, while the Bible makes it clear that demon possession is real, there is no need for a Christian to ever fear such a fate.

Read 1 John 4:4b in the margin and 1 Corinthians 6:19 in your Bible. Restate these truths in your own words.

In what ways can you take comfort in these assurances?

The infinite power and authority of God far surpasses the strength of any demonic being, including Satan himself. When the Holy Spirit of God indwells a Christian, no demon or evil spirit could ever enter. God, as our loving Father and protector, would never allow it.[24] However, the enemy does not give up so easily. He may be unable to inhabit our bodies, but he will stop at nothing to influence our thoughts. This is where the battle is waged, because Satan knows that it is our *thoughts* that determine our *actions*.

The real battle is in the mind, because it is our thoughts that determine our actions.

Pause to Ponder

Ponder the statement that the real battle is in the mind. Do you agree? Why or why not?

Why is meditating on God's Word our best defense against the devil's schemes?

The High Price of Deception

As long as we live in enemy territory, the enemy will do everything he can to try to derail us through deception, temptation, condemnation, and anything else that provides him a foothold in our thoughts.

And when he does, the price we pay is always costly.

I became sexually active by the time I was fourteen years old. When I was fifteen, I was dating a boy who was seventeen and I discovered I was pregnant. I believed the lies that I had no other choice but to have an abortion.[25] Barely six months after the abortion, I began contemplating suicide. By this time, my mother had remarried and we were living in a very large, old house in upstate New York. I remember one afternoon being at home and staring out an upstairs window. As I gazed out the thin, single-paned glass, an idea entered my mind: *If I could just thrust my wrist through the glass, maybe I could cut myself in just the right place and end it all right here, right now*. Thankfully, I never had the courage; but thoughts of suicide still lingered.

"Your enemy the devil prowls around like a roaring lion looking for someone to devour."
—1 Peter 5:8 NIV

A few months later, when no one else was home, I raided my parents' medicine cabinet, taking every bottle of prescription drugs I could find. I then headed downstairs to the liquor cabinet, which was never locked. Taking a bottle of vodka back up to my bedroom, I laid everything out on my desk in front of me. I opened the first bottle of pills. I don't even know what the medication was for. I didn't care. Spilling the contents onto the desk, I then poured vodka into a tall glass . . .

At the time, I did not understand the source of my pain, but it did not matter—I just wanted it to go away. Surely it is only by God's grace that in the end, I did not have the courage to take the pills; instead, I took a pen. Retrieving my little yellow diary from its hiding place, I began to write. The hours seemed like minutes as I furiously scribbled page after page. One year later, for reasons I may never know, I took a pair of scissors and cut out all of those pages. To this day, I

still have that little yellow diary, but the heartrending words that poured from that young girl's soul are lost forever.

Your Turn

As Christians living within an unseen spiritual realm, you and I are going to experience situations where it will take more than positive thinking to get us out. Each of us suffers from blind spots—places in our lives where we fail to recognize, and thereby fail to rest under the protection of, God's authority.

Read Colossians 1:16–17. Rewrite the passage in your own words.

Spend some time in prayer asking God to reveal to you any areas of your life that you tend to regard—whether willfully or in ignorance—as being outside of God's control. Write what He reveals to you and what steps you will take next.

Day Four

Adjusting Your Perspective

"What has been is what will be, and what has been done is what will be done, and there is nothing new under the sun."
—Ecclesiastes 1:9

Yesterday we spent quite some time examining the tremendous suffering of the demon-possessed man, but we only briefly touched on the topic of self-harm or "cutting." Today's lesson begins with this difficult topic. I remember the first time I met someone who shared that she had previously engaged in this tragic behavior. We were taking a class together while in seminary. At first, I was surprised to meet a former "cutter" in seminary. But then I remembered my own past: abortion, promiscuity, drug and alcohol abuse, date rape, divorce. . . .

Sometimes we make the mistake of classifying people into categories based upon what we think they are or are not capable of. However, the challenges and tragedies we face in the world today are nothing new—nor are the ways we respond to them. In the book of Ecclesiastes, God's wise king Solomon reminds us that "there is nothing new under the sun" (1:9). Sadly, this would include the heartbreaking behavior of cutting.

Reread Mark 5:5: "Night and day among the tombs and on the mountains he was always crying out and cutting himself with stones." List all of the reasons this man's suffering and self-mutilation might grieve the heart of God.

Of the reasons you listed, which is most tragic in your opinion? Why?

The Enemy's Delight

As I shared yesterday, I have known deep despair to the point of wanting to take my life. However, because I never engaged in the self-injury practice known today as cutting, I do not claim to understand the kind of torment that causes people to repeatedly physically harm themselves. While I am no expert on the topic, I have done some research as well as talked with people who have suffered in this way. One thing I have found is that this behavior is no respecter of persons. While the specific reasons for cutting are often as varied as the persons themselves, most former or recovering cutters confess that they often cut in order to deflect their thoughts from deeper emotional or psychological pain, such as depression, anger, guilt, loneliness, or self-hate.

While it can be difficult to determine whether any particular case of cutting is directly due to the influence of demonic activity, all self-destructive behaviors, like all sin, result in harm to oneself and others—and this always fills our enemy with delirious delight. Because you and I and every human being are created in the image of God, Satan revels in our misery, harm, and destruction. Whether this comes as a result of cutting, lying, stealing, sexual sin, or something else, it makes no difference to him.

Pause to Ponder

Have you ever been so tortured of soul that you wanted to harm yourself? (Note: self-harm can also include addictions, reckless choices, or other self-destructive behaviors.)

What do you believe led you to that point? Looking back, how do you suppose your suffering grieved the heart of God?

The Danger of Idolatry

Read Leviticus 19:28 and Deuteronomy 14:1. Identify the behavior prohibited by God and what it is associated with.

In biblical times, expressions of mourning for loved ones who had passed away often included wailing, tearing one's garments, covering oneself with ashes, wearing sackcloth, and other traditions. While those in neighboring cultures also practiced cutting themselves in association with mourning for the dead, this particular behavior was strictly prohibited among God's people.

Cutting was also associated with something else. To fully grasp its significance, we need to briefly step back once again into the Old Testament—into the life of one of Israel's kings. The books of 1 and 2 Kings chronicle the reigns of Israel's various kings following the death of King David. While King David's son Solomon started out well, in his later years, he succumbed to idol worship, establishing a tragic pattern for many of the kings of Israel who followed.

Israel's King Ahab married Jezebel, the daughter of the king of Sidon, who was also the high priest of the pagan god Baal.[26]

Read 1 Kings 16:30–33. How is King Ahab described, according to verses 30 and 33?

When Israel was divided into two kingdoms, King Ahab reigned over the northern tribes. During this time, God afflicted the land with a severe famine as judgment for the people's rampant idolatry. After three and a half years, God mercifully sent His prophet Elijah, promising rain (1 Kings 17:1, 18:1–2; see also Deut. 11:16–17 and Luke 4:25). However, the people's hearts remained drawn to idol worship, particularly to the pagan god Baal.[27] Scripture teaches that as part of their worship, the prophets of Baal often cried out and "limped around the altar," probably a form of pagan ritual dance (1 Kings 18:26). Playing on this image, Elijah confronted the people of Israel: "How long will you go limping between two different opinions? If the Lord is God, follow him; but if Baal, then follow him" (1 Kings 18:21).

Pause to Ponder

Describe a time when you were torn between following God and following something or someone that opposed God. How did you move forward? What were the results?

God's prophet Elijah then challenged the prophets of Baal (in front of the watching Israelites) to a contest to reveal whether their god or Elijah's God was real. Each prepared a bull sacrifice. All the people agreed that whichever god consumed the sacrifice by fire was the one true God.

Read 1 Kings 18:25–29. (Optional: read the full story in verses 20–46.) In their efforts to compel their god to act, what did the prophets of Baal do, according to verse 28?

What other observations can you make?

The pagan prophets were quite a spectacle. In addition to their limping and raving, Scripture says they cut themselves *after their custom*. This was not a one-time occurrence, but rather a common practice as part of their ritual worship. We can only imagine the heinous laughter of Satan and his demons as these men, created in the image of God, mutilated themselves, ranting and raving "until the blood gushed out upon them."

The Root of Idolatry

If you asked the average person to describe what comes to mind when they hear the expression "idol worship," what might they say?

"The essence of idolatry is the entertainment of thoughts about God that are unworthy of Him."
—A. W. Tozer

Often when we think of idol worship, our minds conjure up images of ancient times and carved images, but it is so much more. Perhaps A. W. Tozer said it best when he wrote, "The essence of idolatry is the entertainment of thoughts about God that are unworthy of Him."[28] Sin is always rooted in a rebellious heart (Matt. 9:4; Mark 7:21–23), birthing in the mind distorted thoughts of God, which is idolatry.

Therefore, to gain the upper hand, all the enemy needs to do is exploit our pride and rebellion, which slither easily into our minds, distorting our thoughts about God. From there, our thoughts simply determine our actions. The prophets of Baal *believed* that their god required them to mutilate themselves, so they *behaved* accordingly.

Read Mark 5:6–7 (verse 6 is review) and Luke 8:31; then answer the questions that follow.

Speaking through the man, what title did the demons use to address Jesus?

Do you think their use of this title is significant? Why or why not?

What did the demons fear? Rewrite their request in your own words.

Why do you think the demons believed they needed to plead with Jesus?

The Greek verb *horkizo* in Mark 5:7, which is typically translated as "adjure," "implore," or sometimes "beg," is a very strong Greek verb. It means to put someone under oath or make a person swear to something. As aptly expressed in the NIV Bible translation, the demons plead with Jesus, saying, "Swear to God that you will not torture me!" The demons know exactly who Jesus is. They address Him as "Son of the Most High God." They know that if Jesus grants their request, His decision carries the same authority as His Father.

Pause to Ponder

When you consider the magnitude of power that Satan and his demons possess, how do you tend to view it in relation to your own? (Optional: draw an illustration of your thoughts, such as contrasting two lines or circles.)

Now, describe your perception of Satan's power in comparison to God's.

For many of us, our perception of ourselves and the enemy's power over us can leave us vulnerable if, in the midst of these mindsets, we also hold on to an inaccurate view of *God's* power. Suppose you were to mark on a sliding scale your perception of your own power in comparison to the enemy's power and God's power. Perhaps it would look something like the illustration below. We often see ourselves as having little power, God having the greatest power, and the enemy somewhere in between.

Self ·························· **Enemy** ·························· **God**

LEAST POWER — MOST POWER

But we would be wrong. *Perilously wrong.* It is true that Satan and demons have incredible power when compared to our own—angels are mighty beings. However, unlike God, angels, demons, and humans are all creatures. For each one of us, our very existence depends on God. God, however, is uncreated. He exists in a category all by Himself that is infinitely above all we could possibly imagine. Everything in all of creation—whether physical or spiritual—is completely dependent upon Him. He rules the universe and all are in subjection to Him. This is why when demons find themselves in the presence of Almighty God, they cannot help but fall down—they do so filled with rage and hate, but they will bow nonetheless.

To you and me, Satan and his demons are a powerful force and should never be trivialized. But God is God *Most High*—a Hebrew expression conveying the idea that God is above all, He is supreme over all, and He even dwells high above the heavens. He is the infinite, eternal, and all-powerful Ruler of the Universe. Even if we took Satan and all his demons wrapped up together, they would be infinitesimally inferior to the Almighty God. Considering the previous sliding scale example, it is vital that we recognize God does not have "most" power. He holds *all* the power. In fact, He *is* power; that is, nothing has power apart from Him. Any sliver of control or power or authority that we—or even the demons, for that matter—appear to possess is limited, temporary, and entirely due to God's sovereign will, which He always exercises to accomplish His good purposes.

"[A]t the name of Jesus EVERY KNEE WILL BOW, of those who are in heaven and on earth and under the earth, and . . . every tongue will confess that Jesus Christ is Lord."
—Philippians 2:10–11 NASB

God does not have "most" power. He holds *all* the power. In fact, He *is* power.

Your Turn

Do you struggle at times to keep the power of God (and the enemy) in a proper perspective? If so, why do you think that is?

Take some time right now to ask God to help you recognize any beliefs you hold about Him that are unworthy of Him. Write a prayer of confession and repentance in the margin. (Optional: choose one or two Scripture verses that address these erroneous beliefs and commit them to memory.)

Imagine a person who lives her life fully trusting in God's authority. What might that look like? How will you glorify God this week by modeling a life trusting in God's authority?

Day Five

Confronting the Enemy

"Jesus is the way!" These are the words that suddenly pierced the quiet as I sat lazily on the beach, watching the ocean waves. I was enjoying my weekly date with Jesus when on the boardwalk about fifty feet behind me, a man started singing a popular worship song at the top of his lungs. At first, I was delighted. *Preach it!* I thought to myself. But after a few minutes, I sensed something was wrong—very wrong.

He seemed to be blaring the words, not singing them. After listening more intently, I realized the problem: there was no heart in his voice. The man was neither worshiping nor evangelizing. It seemed that his sole purpose was to disrupt, distract, and annoy people. His *words* may have proclaimed God's name and even some spiritual truths, but his voice and behavior gave no honor to God whatsoever. He wasn't singing—he was screaming. He wasn't worshiping—he was *mocking*. I felt my teeth and fists clench as anger swelled within me. . . . It was in that instant that God reminded me of the story in Mark 1.

The Light Bearer's Plunge to Darkness

Near the end of Week One, we explored several accounts of Jesus casting out demons in Mark 1. Scripture teaches that Jesus did not permit the demons to speak *because they knew Him* (Mark 1:32–34). This "knowing" is neither a vague understanding nor a recent revelation. While we do not know precisely when God created angels, Scripture does reveal that they were present at the creation of the physical world (Job 38:4–7).

Because God is holy and good, everything He created was created good, even Satan. "Before he rebelled against God, Satan was Lucifer, or 'light bearer,' the most glorious and beautiful creature God ever made."[29] His name is a reference to the morning star, which is the planet Venus. This star announces the coming of the sun by its reflection of the sun's light. In the same way, Satan at one time served to announce the majestic presence of God by acting as a reflection of God's glory.[30]

However, just as Adam and Eve were created good, *but were not created unchangeably good*, so it was with the angels. At some point before the beginning of time, Satan rejected the truth (John 8:44), fell from heaven (Luke 10:18), and has been sinning ever since (1 John 3:8). Therefore, all angels (including fallen angels) have existed in the presence of God for untold millennia, and they know exactly who Jesus is. However, it seems that Jesus had determined beforehand how and when His identity would be revealed on earth—and this divine message would not enter human history by the mouths of demons.

Lucifer means "light-bearer." It is the Latin name for the planet Venus, the brightest object in our sky apart from the sun and moon. The name is derived from the Hebrew word *helel*, meaning "star" in Isaiah 14:12.[31]

Be Muzzled!

Glance back at Mark 1:24-27. Compare this passage with Mark 4:39-41. What parallels can you discover?

In addition to Jesus's rebuke and the people's response, there is another parallel I'd like you to see that may be less obvious, depending on the English translation you are reading. In Mark 1:25, Jesus commands the demon, "Be silent, and come out of him!" In Greek, the root verb translated "be silent" is *phimoo*, which literally means "to muzzle." That's quite a visual!

The picture of being muzzled is not one of willful obedience, but of bound aggression. It is the identical verb Jesus uses in Mark 4:39 when he commands the violent wind and sea, "Peace! Be still!" or literally, "Silence! Be muzzled!" In both stories, the people are awestruck, marveling, *Who is this?*—for they know that only God has the power to control the wind and the sea.

"[God] commanded and raised the stormy wind, which lifted up the waves of the sea. . . . He made the storm be still, and the waves of the sea were hushed."
—Psalm 107:25, 29

Jesus had already demonstrated His power over disease, handicaps, even demons—and now He reveals His power over nature. These stories serve as a testimony of Jesus's authority as the Son of God. As witnesses of these events, Jesus's disciples have also been being prepared. For over a year, the disciples have observed Jesus's miracles and growing popularity as people came from every corner to be healed by Jesus and hear His message.

Then, just as the crowds began to swell, Jesus leaves the throng behind and decides to take His disciples sailing. We can only guess what the disciples expected to encounter on the other side, but I imagine that a crazed, naked demoniac was not on the list. Just as the physical storm took the disciples by surprise, the spiritual storm that was racing toward them as they reached the shore would surely put their faith to the test.

Pause to Ponder

Think of a time when God led you somewhere unexpected (the destination could be a physical place, but it also could be an experience). What do you suppose God wanted you to learn? What *did* you learn?

A Life Out of Control

If you have not previously read Mark 5:1-20 once all the way through, please do so now to get an overview of the story.

In Mark 5:4, we read that no one had the strength to subdue (or "tame") the man. What comes to mind when you read these words? How do you picture it?

The word translated "subdue" (or "tame") is *damasai* in Greek. It is a rare word in the New Testament, appearing in only one other passage.

Read James 3:7-8. How does this passage shed light on Mark 5:4?

In James 3:7–8, we read that virtually every kind of earthly creature can be tamed. Yet in Mark 5 we encounter the most pitiful creature of all who has been debased to the point that even beasts surpass him. Homeless, friendless, and alienated from society, the tormented man tore his shackles and chains to pieces, but he could not break the chains that held his mind prisoner. Running crazed into the night, his shrieks echoed from the mountaintops, but no one could hear the wails echoing in the prison of his soul. The evidence of deep cuts on the man's broken, bloodied body were plain to everyone, but no one could see the broken, bleeding heart crying out for deliverance—*no one but Jesus.*

Pause to Ponder

While none of us is ever likely to experience the kind of torment this man endured, all of us have experienced suffering. In what ways can you sympathize with the man?

Read Mark 5:6–9. What had Jesus been saying to the demoniac?

Based on the grammar in the original text, it seems that Jesus issued His command more than once. The phrase "Jesus was saying" is in the imperfect verb form in Greek, which means it is a *continuous* (or repeated) action.

Given Jesus's identity, authority, and prior incidents of casting out demons, why do you suppose it was even possible that Jesus's command was not immediately obeyed? (Hint: compare verses 8 and 9.)

When Jesus speaks to the demoniac, the verb "come out" is singular in Greek. Jesus also uses the singular noun "unclean spirit." It seems that the demons, being not one but many, jumped at the chance to exploit an apparent loophole in Jesus's words, but their clever games would not get them far. In fact, they were playing right into Jesus's hands.

Reread the first part of the demons' response in Mark 5:7. Describe the complaint in your own words.

"For the Lord, the Most High, is to be feared, a great king over all the earth."
—Psalm 47:2

Time Is Running Out

The reality is that the demons are seething because Jesus has arrived on their turf.[32] For several thousands of years, they have enjoyed a certain level of freedom. However, when the Son of God set His foot on the earth two thousand years ago, demonic activity seemed to surge to a new level.[33]

Why do you think demonic activity intensified during Jesus's earthly ministry?

Although the demons bow before Jesus (verse 6), it is not out of reverence. Demons cannot help but tremble in the presence of their Judge,[34] whose very sight fills them with dread for the torment and hellfire that awaits them.[35] Filled with hate and rebellion, they even go so far as to challenge Jesus's right to interfere with them: "What have you to do with me, Jesus, Son of the Most High God?"

Compare Matthew 8:29 with Mark 5:7. What additional detail does Matthew include in the demoniac's response?

What may this additional detail be referring to? List as many possibilities as you can think of.

In the New Testament, there are two Greek words for time. *Chronos* is quantitative and refers to chronological time measured in days and hours and minutes. The other word is *kairos*, which is not quantitative but qualitative. *Kairos* relates to a proper, suitable, or opportune time. This is the idea found in Ecclesiastes 3:1–8, which begins, "For everything there is a season, and a time for every matter under heaven." A simple illustration can also be found right in our kitchens: when a green banana turns yellow, the right "time" to eat it has arrived.

In Matthew 8:29, the demons complain that they are being tortured before the appointed time (*kairos*). Most biblical scholars hold that this relates to the final judgment, the arrival of which God alone knows. Nevertheless, regarding that judgment, there is no question as to the fate of the devil and his angels. Jesus Himself said that hell was created precisely with them in mind (Matt. 25:41). What irony! The demons were afraid that Jesus would banish them into eternal torment *before the time*, yet all the while they would gladly torture and torment this poor man for as long as they could.[36]

Your Turn

Read Colossians 1:13 at least two times and at least once out loud. What are the only two realms in which a person can exist?

As a child of God, what difference has it made to you to be:

Delivered from the domain of darkness?

Transferred to the kingdom of Jesus, the Son of God?

Write a prayer of gratitude below.

Lesson Summary

What Scripture, statement, or thought was most significant to you this week? Write it down and then reword it into a prayer of response to God.

Notes

[1] Johnston Cheney and Stanley Ellisen, *Jesus Christ: The Greatest Life* (Eugene, OR: Paradise Publishing, 1999), 26, 45.

[2] Study Notes, *The ESV Study Bible* (Wheaton, IL: Crossway Bibles, 2008), 1826.

[3] "Mark 4:35-41", *Holman Bible Handbook*, ed. D. S. Dockery (Nashville: Holman Bible Publishers, 1992), 573.

[4] The ESV, NKJV, KJV, and NIV all translate the adjective as "so afraid"; the NASB and NLT leave out the emphatic "so." Nevertheless, the adjective in Greek is in the nominative case, which means that the emphasis is on the subject of the sentence, which in this case is the disciples. To accomplish this in English, the word "so" has been added by some translators.

[5] Jesus's disciples ("the Twelve," as well as other followers) each joined Jesus during His earthly ministry at various times. For the purposes of this exercise, we begin our chronology

after Andrew, Peter (Simon), Philip, and Nathanael (four of the Twelve) begin to follow Jesus (John 1:35–51).

[6] "The Ten Plagues of Egypt," *Nelson's Complete Book of Bible Maps and Charts: Old and New Testaments*, revised and updated ed. (Nashville: Thomas Nelson, 1996).

[7] Study Notes, *ESV Study Bible* (Wheaton, IL: Crossway Bibles, 2008), 1901.

[8] A. W. Tozer, *The Knowledge of the Holy* (New York: HarperOne, 1961), 83.

[9] H. R. Jones, *A Study Commentary on Job* (Darlington, England: Evangelical Press, 2007), 58–59.

[10] Notes for Job 1:18–19, *The NET Bible* (Richardson, TX: Biblical Studies Press, 2006).

[11] H. D. Buckwalter, "Gerasa, Gerasene, Gergesa, Gergesene," in *Baker Encyclopedia of the Bible*, vol. 1 (Grand Rapids, MI: Baker Book House, 1988), 857.

[12] C. W. Hensley, "Gadara, Gadarenes," in *Baker Encyclopedia of the Bible*, vol. 1 (Grand Rapids, MI: Baker Book House, 1988), 827.

[13] A few manuscripts of Mark's Gospel record the location as being the region of *Gergesenes*. Gergesa was a very small town and, like Gadara, it was located on the eastern side of the Sea of Galilee. As such, it also would be considered in the same general vicinity of Gadara as well as the wider region of Gerasa.

[14] Compare the stories of the blind men in Matthew 9:27–31 and 20:29–34 with Mark 10:46–52 and Luke 18:35–43; the colt and donkey in Matthew 21:1–11 with Mark 11:1–11 and Luke 19:29–38; and the demoniacs in Matthew 8:28–34 with Mark 5:1–17 and Luke 8:26–39.

[15] J. P. Lange and P. Schaff, *A Commentary on the Holy Scriptures: Matthew* (Bellingham, WA: Logos Bible Software, 2008), 164.

[16] ESV, NASB, NCV, NIV, NLT, HCSV, YLT

[17] NKJV, KJV, ASV, MSB

[18] R. Hawker, *Poor Man's New Testament Commentary: Matthew–John,* vol. 1 (Bellingham, WA: Logos Bible Software, 2013), 234.

[19] D. E. Garland, *Mark* (Grand Rapids, MI: Zondervan Publishing House, 1996), 203.

[20] William MacDonald, *Believer's Bible Commentary: Old and New Testaments*, ed. A. Farstad (Nashville: Thomas Nelson, 1995), 1332. This quote was originally found in *Scripture Union Notes.*

[21] William Barclay, *The New Daily Study Bible: The Gospel of Mark* (Edinburgh: Saint Andrew Press, 2001), 136.

[22] Joel P. Jupp, "Ancestor Worship," *The Lexham Bible Dictionary,* ed. John D. Barry et al. (Bellingham, WA: Lexham Press, 2016).

[23] Tony Evans, *The Truth about Angels and Demons* (Chicago: Moody Publishers, 2005), 12–13.

[24] R. Dean Jr. and T. Ice, *What the Bible Teaches about Spiritual Warfare* (Grand Rapids, MI: Kregel Publications, 2000), 134.

[25] Abortion is a deep and painful wound that has affected many. If you (or someone you love) has suffered the heartbreak of abortion, I invite you to read my personal story, which I share in my Bible study *Worthy of Love: A Journey of Hope and Healing after Abortion.*

[26] R. R. Losch, *All the People in the Bible: An A–Z Guide to the Saints, Scoundrels, and Other Characters in Scripture* (Grand Rapids, MI: Eerdmans, 2008), 216.

[27] It seems that the people were trying to have it both ways. They worshiped God to please His prophets, but they worshiped Baal to please Jezebel (the wife of Israel's King Ahab), since she held much power and influence in the kingdom. Matthew Henry, *Matthew Henry's Commentary on the Whole Bible* (Peabody, MA: Hendrickson, 1994), 510.

[28] A. W. Tozer, *The Knowledge of the Holy* (New York: HarperOne, 1961), 3.

[29] Evans, *Truth about Angels and Demons*, 13.

[30] Dean and Ice, *What the Bible Teaches*, 45–46.

[31] D. H. Wheaton, "Lucifer," in *New Bible Dictionary*, 3rd ed., ed. D. R. W. Wood et al. (Downers Grove, IL: InterVarsity Press, 1996), 702.

[32] When referring to "enemy territory" or similar expressions, it is important to keep in mind that God is the rightful King over all the earth (Ps. 47). Although God delegated authority to humanity who in turn forfeited it over to Satan, the enemy's reign is both limited and temporary.

[33] Not only does the Bible reveal a stark contrast between the level of overt demonic activity in the Old Testament as compared to the New, but even more, the demonic activity portrayed in the Gospels (which focus on Jesus's earthly ministry) far exceeds that which is presented in the remainder of the New Testament.

[34] See John 5:22 and Matthew 28:18.

[35] J. Calvin and W. Pringle, *Commentary on a Harmony of the Evangelists Matthew, Mark, and Luke*, vol. 1 (Bellingham, WA: Logos Bible Software, 2010), 431.

[36] Allen Ross, "The Demons and the Pigs," Bible.org, March 22, 2006, https://bible.org/seriespage/demons-and-pigs-matthew-828-34.

NOTES

EXPERIENCING GOD'S RESTORATION

WEEK FOUR

THIS WEEK, WE WILL MARVEL AT THE DEPTH OF ONE MAN'S torment and the power of God's restoration. With just a word:

- A demoniac becomes a disciple.
- A house of demons becomes a dwelling for the Living God.
- The chained becomes a champion of good news.

DAY ONE

Recognizing the Spiritual Battle

I am not certain when I started to break inside. Keeping secrets changes a person. And surely no one wanted to hear about my abortion or suicidal thoughts. Even if someone had been willing to listen, I doubt I would have found the courage to speak up. It did not take long after that season before I began hanging with the wrong crowd. I had already started drinking by the time I was sixteen. By seventeen, I was in nightclubs abusing drugs and alcohol—an effective escape from my painful thoughts.

Then one night, a man slipped me a date-rape drug. Even today, the flashbacks remain seared in my memory. He drove me to a dark, secluded place, parked his shiny red truck, and almost immediately started tugging at my clothing. It was then that I realized I couldn't move. I couldn't speak. I couldn't scream. I could smell his alcohol-tainted breath on my face as I slipped in and out of consciousness. But that is not what I remember most from that night. It was what I saw when I momentarily looked out the passenger window. In the clearing some distance away, I saw a man dressed in some kind of uniform. Military? Police? Though it was dark outside, the man was surrounded by a soft glow of light. He just stood there.

Why won't you help me!? my mind screamed as my heart pleaded for rescue. . . . But he never moved. He never came. Looking back, I don't know if the man I saw was a dream, a hallucination, or an angel of God. I never told anyone what happened to me that night. More shame. More secrets. More pieces of my heart retreating into darkness . . .

A few months later, I graduated from high school with honors. No one knew the double life I was leading. Everyone saw what they wanted to see. My family saw their straight-A student heading to college. My friends saw a fun, confident party girl. Predatory men saw an opportunity. But when I looked in the mirror, I saw only an empty shell. For years, when I would think back on that night, I felt betrayed—both by the man who violated me and by the man who stood by and did nothing, whether he was real or imagined. I know my reckless lifestyle was partly to blame, but the man who raped me had committed a serious crime. *Where was God that night?*

It's a fair question, especially when we look around at a world where evil appears to have the upper hand. Yet, today, I can look back and marvel at all the ways God protected me that night. I was not kidnapped. I was not left in the woods or on the side of the road. I could have died, but God spared my life. Though I suffered, God is not to blame for the evil I suffered at the hands of that depraved man. Perhaps author C. S. Lewis explained it best when he wrote, "God created things which [have] free will. . . . [F]ree will is what has made evil possible. Why, then, did God give [us] free will? Because free will, though it makes evil possible, is also the only thing that makes possible any love or goodness or joy worth having."[1]

"Free will, though it makes evil possible, is also the only thing that makes possible any love or goodness or joy worth having."
—C. S. Lewis

When I consider my past sufferings—whether I suffered as an innocent victim or due to my own poor choices—I realize that all I really wanted was for someone to see me for me. For someone to value me as a person and love me for who I was created to be. Sadly, by the time my life began spinning out of control, even I did not know who that was.

Pause to Ponder

God knew what would happen when He created humanity with a free will; apparently He thought it worth the risk. Try to imagine a world where neither free will nor evil exists. Compare and contrast this with our world in which both free will and evil exist. If you could live in one world or the other, which would you choose? Why?

Sizing Up the Enemy

"What is your name?" Jesus asked.

"My name is Legion, for we are many."

It was as if the identity of the man possessed by the legion had all but disappeared, but Jesus saw what no one else could see. He saw the precious soul trapped inside what had become an empty shell of a human being. Only Jesus could hear the man's cries echoing from the depths of his prison: Is anyone out there? Does anyone care? The answer is *yes!* Jesus hears your heart—the one He created—crying out for deliverance. He feels your pain, and He knows your fears and failures. He has come to rescue you from your torment and helplessness. Jesus sees you, dear one; He sees *behind the seen.*

Jesus hears your heart—the one *He* created—crying out for deliverance. He feels your pain, and He knows your fears and failures. He has come to rescue you from your torment and helplessness.

What reason might Jesus have had for asking the demoniac his name? List as many possibilities as you can think of.

This is the only time in Scripture when Jesus asks a demon its name. A legion in the Roman army was a regiment of soldiers up to six thousand men. Based on Jesus's prior encounters with demons and, more importantly, His authority as the Son of God, it was not necessary for Jesus to ask the demon his name in order to cast him out—whether the demon was one or one thousand. Nevertheless, Jesus allowed this exchange in order to expose the depth of horror that the man was suffering—and the depth of His compassion to deliver him. Jesus used the demons' defiance to unveil the severity of the man's condition. He did this not only for the man himself to see, but also for Jesus's disciples to see, who were likely standing nearby in stunned silence.

Glance back at Mark 4:38–40 and 5:6–7, then complete the sentences by filling in the missing words or phrases. I completed two for you.

"' *Teacher* , don't you care that we ________________?' . . . He said to them, 'Why are you so ____________? Have you still no ____________?'" (Mark 4:38, 40).

"And when he saw Jesus from afar, he ran and *fell down* before him. And crying out with a loud voice, he said, 'What have you to do with me, Jesus, _________________________________?'" (Mark 5:6–7).

Compare and contrast the titles that the disciples and the demons use to address Jesus, along with each of their responses to Jesus's presence. What conclusions can you draw?

Marveling at Your God

Read the Scriptures listed in the chart. For each passage, complete the table by writing each title for God in the second column. In the third column, write each attribute, virtue, or role of God. I filled in a few to get you started.

Scripture	Titles for God	God's Attributes/ Virtues/Roles
Psalm 57:1–3	*God* *God Most High*	

Psalm 89:8–11		*Almighty* *Faithful* *Ruler over creation* *Warrior/crushes enemies* *Creator* *Sovereign over the universe*
Isaiah 9:6–7		

Pause to Ponder

Slowly ponder the words in the table, which presents only a fraction of God's titles and attributes.

Which one stirs your heart the most right now? Why?

When you think about God, which attribute comes to mind *least* often? Why do you think that is?

Oh, the glorious names and attributes of God! In just a few verses, we are reminded of His love, mercy, power, protection, sovereignty, salvation, and promise to destroy our enemies. The fact that the demons in Mark 5 used the expression "Most High God" is very significant. This title, including any variants such as "God Most High," is an ancient name used by both Jews and Gentiles[2] to identify the one, true, living God of Israel and distinguish Him from all false gods.[3] The demons may be seething on the inside, but, like it or not, they have no choice but to acknowledge Jesus as the Son of the *Most High God*.[4]

The title "LORD of Hosts," though not found in the story in Mark 5, is "a phrase describing Yahweh's role as the Lord of the heavenly armies, the commander of the cosmic forces, the head of the divine council, and the leader of Israel's army."[5] In the presence of Jesus, all the pomp and arrogance of this renegade army of demons comes crashing to the ground as they bow at His feet with their faces in the dust.

Their rebellious complaints testify that their confession of Jesus as Son of the Most High God was not made from choice, but was drawn out of them by force.[6] Coming face-to-face with Jesus, the demons knew full well that regardless of their numbers, they were no match for the King of kings and Lord of lords (Rev. 19:11–16).

"And the armies of heaven . . . were following him on white horses. . . . On his robe and on his thigh he has a name written, King of kings and Lord of lords."
—Revelation 19:14, 16

Pause to Ponder

How often do you ponder various titles and names of God?

weekly monthly rarely never

How might your prayers change if you incorporated more time mediating on God's titles, such as Most High God or LORD of hosts or King of kings and Lord of lords?

Bargaining with Your Maker

At the end of last week's lesson, we examined the demons' first request: that they not be cast into eternal torment *before the time*. They recognized Jesus as the One who will execute their final judgment, but they were clinging to their diabolical existence on earth for as long as they could.

Read the demons' second request in Mark 5:10. Why do you think they did not want to leave the area?

Read the demons' third request in Mark 5:11–12. Why might the demons have sought to enter the pigs?

Try to picture this from the demons' perspective; imagine what they might be thinking. This is Gentile territory! *Our* territory! We're free! There is no worship of the One True God going on here. And the pigs! God declared pigs unclean for the Jews centuries ago. Ha! Here they flourish in abundance in all of their delicious mud and filth. Yes, indeed—an exquisite reservoir for shameless pagan sacrifices. Oh, and don't make us leave our hillside of graves, gorging on an endless swell of dead bodies—*What have you to do with us, Jesus, Son of the Most High God?*

A pathetic battle of wits ensues as the demons immediately resort to begging, trying to bargain with Jesus even though they know that without His permission, they have no power, no rights, and no say. They know Jesus will never allow them to enter another human host, so in desperation, they plead to enter the pigs. In the end, Jesus evicts the demons from their human host by sending them into the large herd of pigs that plunge into the sea and drown—a precursor to the demons' ultimate fate, which we will explore further in tomorrow's lesson.

Your Turn

Glance back at the table you completed on pages 122–23. On a note card, write one or two titles of God that you have not pondered lately. On the other side, write one or two attributes of God that seldom come to mind. Meditate on these truths over the next two weeks. Toward the end of Week Five, I will ask you to return here and record what you have discovered.

Day Two
Previewing God's Judgment

When we consider the power of Satan and his demons, it is almost comical that when we finally get a good glimpse into their behavior, we find hissing, cowering beggars. *What do you want with us, Jesus? Swear to God you won't torture us!*

Don't send us into the abyss! Let us stay here, we beg you! Send us into the pigs; let us enter them! Please!

Read Mark 5:13. List every action that occurs in the text.

How do the events in Mark 5:13 further reveal the extent of the man's suffering?

Picture the scene: seeing that Jesus had not come to execute the demons' final judgment—after all, it was *before the time*—and, being forced to abandon their human host, the demons immediately looked around for a new victim. For another opportunity to inflict chaos and torment on God's beloved creation. There on the hillside, a huge herd of pigs is leisurely grazing on grass, plants, roots, insects, and anything else it can find.

Spying the pigs, the demons squeal with delight as they present Jesus with their request. If they could not destroy the man, perhaps they could find a way to entice the *entire town* to curse God![7] Jesus responds with a single word: "Go!" (Matt. 8:32). All at once, the herd is thrown into a panic. Squealing in terror, kicking dirt and grass into the air, the pigs stampede right off the edge of the cliff, plunging to their deaths in the water below.

Why might Jesus have given the demons permission to enter the pigs? List as many reasons as you can think of.

Counting the Cost

When I visited the county fair each year as a young adult, my favorite exhibit was always the pen of baby "piggies." Just thinking back on them makes me smile. We live in a culture that is nearly obsessed with animals. Pampered pets are everywhere. There are zoos to visit, not to mention animal movies, videos, and TV shows. In my leisure time, one of my top choices for video entertainment is nature documentaries. I've watched countless shows on every kind of creature. I will simply never tire of marveling at God's astounding creation.

So it may not be surprising that some have cast doubt on Jesus's compassion for allowing these helpless creatures to be destroyed. Others question His wisdom for such a waste. However, Scripture teaches that God delights in *all* His creatures (Gen. 1:31).

"And God saw everything that he had made, and behold, it was very good."

—Genesis 1:31a

Imagine that you are the demon-possessed man's parent, child, or sibling standing nearby when Jesus comes on the scene. The demons, speaking through the man, beg Jesus to send them into the pigs. How would you react? What would you say to Jesus?

The problem with focusing on the loss of the pigs is that when we do, we lose sight of what matters most. If the man were our father or brother or son, we would be begging Jesus to rescue him, *no matter the cost*. And when He did, we would be so overcome with joy and gratitude, we wouldn't even give the pigs a second thought. How could we when a human soul created in God's own image was just delivered from unspeakable torment? The reality is that Jesus is exercising the deepest compassion by declaring one lost man more valuable than two thousand pigs. Theologian R. C. Sproul writes, "Only in a culture of death, where human life is denigrated, do people value animals more than people."[8]

"'Of how much more value is a man than a sheep!'"

—Matthew 12:12

Pause to Ponder

Consider the quote by R. C. Sproul above. Do you agree? Why or why not? In what ways have you observed his hypothesis exhibited in our culture?

Clinging to Faith

Jesus's decision to grant the demons' request does not mean for a single moment that He is giving in to the demons or trying to make the best of a bad situation. Jesus knows *exactly* what He is doing. To see this more clearly, we will once again take a look at the story of Job.

Read Job 1:22, which summarizes Job's response to the first round of painful loss he suffered. Now read Job 2:1-10. How did Job respond to Satan's next attack?

Compare Job's two responses with Satan's words in Job 1:11 and 2:5. What conclusions can you draw?

If you were to read the entire book of Job, you would discover times when Job wrestled with his feelings about God, even questioning God's fairness (Job 9:17). Yet even in the midst of unspeakable sorrow, Job never cursed or denied Him. Though Job wrestled with his faith in God, *God never lost faith in Job*. As my friend and author Bruce Martin writes in his excellent book *Desperate for Hope*, "God bet the farm on Job because He believed in him."[9]

In the end, God gave Job twice what he had before, Job enjoyed God's blessings to a ripe old age, God was glorified—and Satan slithered away with rotten egg on his face.

Though Job wrestled with his faith in God, God never lost faith in Job.

Twice God gave Satan permission to test His servant, and twice Satan thought he had Job beat—but both times he was wrong. In the same way, Jesus gave the demons permission to do as they asked but, just as in the story of Job, it did not end at all as they had imagined it would.

An Army of *Locusts*?

Let's look at one other Old Testament story to see what parallels and insights we can discover. It is the Exodus—perhaps one of the most famous stories of God's rescue. You may already be familiar with the story: in response to Egypt's cruel, slave-driving pharaoh, God inflicted ten plagues on the Egyptians[10]—each seemingly more destructive or ominous than the last. But there is one plague in particular that I want to focus on: a plague that serves as a parallel to our story of Legion. The plague of locusts.

In the Bible, locusts often represent catastrophic destruction and are even described in military terms (Joel 2:25; Prov. 30:27). In Joel 2:25, God describes locusts as "my great army."

Read Exodus 10:19. What happened to the army of locusts in the end? Be specific.

After the final plague, Pharaoh let the Israelites go free, but he later changed his mind. Leading his massive army, Pharaoh pursued the Israelites into the wilderness until the people were trapped between his forces and the immense Red Sea.

With Pharaoh's army racing toward them, and water stretching endlessly to their right and to their left, the Israelites were trapped.

Read Exodus 13:17–18 and 14:1–4. Who positioned the Israelites in a place where they were utterly defenseless and why?

Read Exodus 14:10–11. What did the people's fear reveal about their hearts? (Hint: compare this to the disciples' fear in Mark 4:38.)

Read Exodus 14:13–14, which is printed below. Put a circle around each word or phrase representing the people's responsibility, and underline each word or phrase representing the Lord's responsibility.

> And Moses said to the people, "Fear not, stand firm, and see the salvation of the LORD. . . . For the Egyptians whom you see today, you shall never see again. The LORD will fight for you, and you have only to be silent."

Pause to Ponder

Of the responsibilities you circled in the previous passage, which do you struggle with the most when you come against trials or attack? Why do you think that is?

Perhaps you are familiar with the rest of the story: God parts the waters of the Red Sea, enabling the Israelites to cross over on dry ground, but the Egyptian army rushes in after them.

"Some trust in chariots and some in horses, but we trust in the name of the LORD our God."
—Psalm 20:7

Read Exodus 14:27–28 and compare it with Exodus 10:19. What similarities can you discover?

In both events, God drove the enemy forces into the sea, and Scripture specifically emphasizes the fact that *not one was left*. (The Hebrew expression is the same in both passages.) The army of locusts served as a warning—a precursor to what would happen to Pharaoh's army.

Now let's compare the Exodus story with the story of Legion. Glance back at Exodus 14:10-11 and 27-28 and Mark 5:13. Then answer the questions that follow.

In the end, what happened to:

The army of locusts?

The army of Pharaoh?

The pigs possessed by a legion of demons?

Based on these answers, what can you infer will be the ultimate fate of the legion, along with Satan and all the rest of the demons?

What effect do you suppose witnessing the pigs being destroyed might have had on the healed man?

Just as the army of locusts served to foreshadow what would happen to Pharaoh's army, the herd of drowned pigs likewise foreshadows what will ultimately happen to the legion of demons. In fact, Scripture promises that at the final judgment, Satan (and, by association, *all* demons) will be cast into the "lake of fire" (Rev. 20:10). When Jesus casts out the legion of demons into the pigs, which then plunge into the sea and drown, He provides a visible demonstration of His authority—and a precursor to what will happen to these demons on the Day of Judgment. And just like Pharaoh's army, *not one will be left*.

But the demons were not the only ones in this story—above all else, Jesus was on a rescue mission.

Your Turn

As Christians, all of us will experience times when we come under attack—whether through persecution (2 Cor. 4:8-10; Luke 6:27-36), temptation (James

1:12–15), or testing (Luke 22:31–32). In these times, if your thoughts are anchored on the truths that *God is sovereign* and *Satan is doomed*, what impact might it have on:

Your prayer life?

Your outlook in this situation?

Your walk with God?

Your witness as a Christ-follower?

Write a prayer of gratitude as God leads you.

DAY THREE
Encountering the Resistance

Earlier in this week's lesson, we uncovered various parallels and contrasts in the story of Legion, such as:

- The disciples' fear of drowning and the demons' fear of judgment
- The disciples' lack of faith and the demons' submission to Jesus's authority
- The disciples calling Jesus "teacher" and the demons calling Him "Son of the Most High God"

Let's see what other contrasts we can discover as we move forward through the story.

Read Mark 5:14-15 and Luke 8:35. In the space below, list everything the text reveals about the man who had been delivered from his torment (you do not need to include the Scripture references unless you choose).

Before Demons Cast Out	After Demons Cast Out
Violent; ran wild (Matt. 8:28; Luke 8:29)	
Wore no clothes (Luke 8:27)	
Lived among the tombs (Mark 5:3; Luke 8:27)	
People posted a guard and tried to bind him with shackles and chains (Mark 5:4; Luke 8:29)	
Cried out and cut himself with stones (Mark 5:5)	

Glance back at Mark 4:37-41. In the space that follows each pair of descriptions outlined below, note the similarities between them.

- The storm's behavior before Jesus's rebuke and man's behavior before Jesus arrives (Mark 5:2-5)
- The storm's behavior after Jesus's rebuke and the man's behavior after Jesus casts out the legion (Mark 5:15)
- The disciples' response to the sudden change and the townspeople's response to the sudden change (Mark 5:15)

"Why are you so afraid? Have you still no faith?"
—Mark 4:40

It is interesting to note that in Mark 4:40–41, the words translated "afraid" and "fear" are not rooted in the same Greek word. In verse 41, we read that the disciples were "filled with great fear." The Greek root word for "fear" in this verse (as well as in Mark 5:15) is *phobos*, which is where we get the English word "phobia." However, Jesus does not use this word when He asks His disciples, "Why are you so afraid?" The Greek word in verse 40 is *deilos*, which includes the idea of being timid or cowardly.

How does this type of fear (cowardice) shed light on the connection Jesus makes between *fear* and *faith* in verse 40?

What principles can you apply to your own life?

The Danger of Ignorance

I'll never forget the night many years ago. I was sharing a home with two dear friends—a husband and wife ten years my senior who, to this day, are like an older brother and sister to me. I had gone to sleep, but I woke perhaps an hour or two later from a terrifying dream. It was nothing like the nightmares I suffered decades earlier that fed on my fears of abuse, which God, in His mercy, had taken away. This was entirely new—and horrifyingly insidious. In the dream, images flashed in my mind, one after the other, of blood, hell, and all kinds of horrors. I had no clue what brought them on. Unable to sleep, I got up to go to the kitchen. I found my friends still awake and quietly reading in the living room.

"What's wrong?" they asked.

"I had a terrifying dream of gory images flashing in my mind, one after another. Whenever I close my eyes, the images keep coming back. I can't sleep!" (Clearly, I had forgotten my friend's advice years earlier about praying that God would take my nightmares away. How quickly we forget!)

My friends reminded me that I belonged to Jesus and was living for Him; Satan could not lay a finger on me without God's permission. As a result, he could only resort to flashing pictures at me. That night, it was ghastly scenes of horror, but he could have pulled out all kinds of pictures from his vile bag of tricks, such as reminders of my past sins, regrets, irrational fears, or anything else that might succeed in shaking my faith, or at least my peace.

I am a very visual person. As I considered my friends' comments, the scene suddenly came into focus. I imagined myself in a protective enclosure surrounded by impenetrable glass. Outside, Satan stood clutching a huge stack of pictures underneath one arm while pathetically throwing them at the glass walls with the other, one by one. Unable to come near me, all he could do was hiss and scream and throw those pictures. *Look at this! And this! And how about this!* As I envisioned the scene in my mind, it nearly became comical. I thanked my friends, went back to bed, and slept soundly the rest of the night.

Sometimes we just need a little perspective.

If fear is an arrow, ignorance is the bow.

The Weapon of Fear

If fear is an arrow, ignorance is the bow. When it comes to spiritual battles, perhaps one of the enemy's greatest assets is our own ignorance, which he gladly uses against us to incite fear in our hearts. And we suffer not only in our periodic failure to fully appreciate the infinite, eternal, Almighty God who holds the entire universe in His hands, but also in our inflated view of the enemy's power.

Most of us tend to err in one direction or the other. At times, we might be like the disciples who ran to Jesus but feared He was not enough. At other times, our minds may dwell too much on the enemy, fixed on his fearsome power (when compared to humans) and the suffering we believe he has inflicted. Either way, the fallout of our ignorance will lead to fear, anxiety, poor choices, and so much more.

"Thus says the LORD, the King of Israel and his Redeemer, the LORD of hosts: 'I am the first and I am the last; besides me there is no god.'" —Isaiah 44:6

PAUSE TO PONDER

How about you? When you face spiritual battles, on which side of the spectrum do you tend to err more: an inadequate view of God's power or an overinflated view of Satan's power? Mark an X on the line below.

too little faith in God's power ______________________________ too much faith in Satan's power

In truth, the two ends of the spectrum are really two sides of the same dangerous coin. No matter which end of the spectrum each of us tends to lean, the solution is the same: to strengthen our understanding of *who God is.*[11] Only then will everything else—including our view of Satan—fall into place.

There is only one way to combat fear, which is to expose it for what it really is: unbelief.[12] As mentioned earlier, some fears are rooted in ignorance, such as who God really is and how He acts toward us. Others are fed by an overinflated view of or preoccupation with Satan or demonic powers in general. Then there are fears rooted in sin, such as fear of what it will cost us to move forward with God. When we cling to a sin we refuse to surrender, we expose the war still raging in our hearts—we expose the enemy's lies that try to convince us that God is not enough.

There is only one way to combat fear, which is to expose it for what it really is: unbelief.

Exposing the Truth

So far in this week's lesson, we have explored several reasons Jesus allowed the demons to enter the pigs. In Day One, we realized that the events served to expose the severity of the man's torment. In Day Two, we learned that the destruction of the pigs highlights the demons' future judgment and ultimate fate. Today, we will discover a third reason Jesus allowed the demons to enter the pigs.

Read Mark 5:16. Then complete the verse by filling in the blanks.

> "And those who had seen it described to them what had happened to the ______________________________ and to the ________."

Read Mark 5:17 and glance back at Mark 5:10–11. What parallel words, phrases, or concepts can you discover between Mark 5:16–17 and 5:10–11?

Why do you think the townspeople asked Jesus to leave? List as many reasons as you can think of.

Compare the townspeople's request in Mark 5:17 with the demons' request in 5:10. How might the demons' motivations be connected to the underlying heart condition of the townspeople?

Pause to Ponder

> Think of a time in your life when you wanted God to leave you alone, or you insisted on going your own way without God. What may have been your underlying motives? What were the results? What did you learn?

Read the following two passages. Briefly describe the conflict taking place.

Luke 13:10–17

Acts 16:16–39

What parallels can you discover in these stories as compared to what we read in Mark 5:15–17?

What principles can you glean concerning the hearts of people in general, based on these passages?

"With the merciful you show yourself merciful . . . and with the crooked you make yourself seem tortuous."
—Psalm 18:25–26

It doesn't take much for a person's true colors to be exposed. Threaten their power, position, or possessions, and you will quickly discover where their true allegiance lies. Just as the synagogue rulers cared more about an ox than a "daughter of Abraham," and the slave owners cared more about money than a girl's tortured soul, the townspeople in Mark 5 cared more about a herd of pigs than a fellow human being. A man that they had tried to keep from harming himself and others has finally been set free from unspeakable pain and torment. Yet, upon seeing the man restored, the people ignored this loving act of mercy and decided they want nothing to do with Jesus. One commentary author summarizes it this way: "So long as men believe that the kingdom of God is opposed to their interest, either of a public or private nature, they are prepossessed by a depraved and carnal fear, and have no [desire] for his grace."[13]

This is the third reason Jesus allowed demons to enter the pigs: it served to expose the hard hearts of the people. Instead of seeing Jesus as kind and merciful, He was seen as severe and cruel. Refusing to see that He came with love and mercy, the people perceived only anger and judgment. As a result, they did everything they could to drive Him from their presence. After all, the pigs would have fetched no small sum for countless pagan sacrifices and festivals. Had they invited Jesus to stay, surely there were others in their midst who might also have been cured of disease, handicap, or demons. But none of that mattered to them. In the end, "they are more disturbed by the presence and power of God than by a legion of devils."[14]

Your Turn

Looking back on your life before you became a Christian, where would you say most of your fears were rooted? Ignorance or inadequate view of God? Inflated view or preoccupation with Satan or demonic activity? Sin? Circumstances? Something else?

How about today?

Are your answers different? Share your thoughts.

Spend some time in prayer asking God to gently expose the roots of any fears that currently have a hold on you. Write what He reveals to you and what steps you will take next.

DAY FOUR
Embracing a New Identity

"[A]ny one of you who does not renounce all that he has cannot be my disciple." —Luke 14:33

"Count the cost." As a Christ-follower, you have probably heard this expression at one time or another. Usually, it is spoken in reference to what it means to be a follower of Jesus and to live for Him (Luke 14:25–33).[15] But those who joyfully embrace Jesus as Lord are not the ones who actually pay a cost for following Him. Oswald Chambers writes, "If we are in love with our Lord, obedience does not cost us anything, it is a delight, but it costs those who do not love Him a good deal. . . . If we obey God, [we can trust that] He will look after those who have suffered the consequences of our obedience."[16] This doesn't mean, of course, that obedience is never painful, only that it costs nothing that we, as followers of Christ, are not already willing to sacrifice as the Holy Spirit enables and empowers us.

Glance back at Mark 5:11-17, then answer the questions that follow.

Who paid the price (suffered loss) as a result of the man being freed from the demons?

How does this shed light on the people's resistance toward Jesus?

List everything you can think of that the townspeople may have forfeited by sending Jesus away. Which loss, in your opinion, is most tragic?

Pause to Ponder

When you became a Christ-follower, what resistance did you encounter? What price did others pay, such as friends or family members, as a result of your changed life?

Read Mark 5:18. What did Jesus do in response to the people begging Him to leave?

What might His response reveal about His character?

A New Beginning

Imagine for a moment that you are the healed man. You've spent what probably feels like an eternity chained in darkness, tormented by death and demons. Then suddenly a legion of angry demons is ripped from your being and cast away from you forever. You fall to your knees, stunned by the sudden calm. Then you look up and gaze into the eyes of Love—your Savior who rescued you. And in those eyes, you search, but cannot find any blame or disgust or condemnation—not a trace of judgment for the sins you know you bear. Suddenly, people come running—your neighbors, perhaps old friends. . . . Surely they will rejoice with you! They will see this Jesus for the love and mercy He poured out by rescuing your mind, body, and soul. But after learning what had happened, the people beg Jesus, *Please leave! We don't want you here!*

Incredible! Instead of embracing Jesus, the people don't want anything to do with Him. He is interfering with their cherished pagan worship, and they just want things to go back to normal. They had come to accept a Legion living in their graveyard. They couldn't chain him, but they found a way to coexist with him.

Pause to Ponder

Today, you and I live in a world that is pleased to coexist with evil; but what about us—those whom God set apart to "shine as lights in the world" (Phil. 2:15)? In what ways have we, as Christians, become content to coexist with evil?

Imagine once again that you are the healed man. How might the townspeople's response to Jesus and your deliverance affect you? What might you be thinking or feeling?

We can only guess what went through his mind, but I can picture him thinking, *No! My ears must be playing tricks on me! Did the people just ask my Rescuer to leave? After all I've been through? No, it can't be true! Oh, Jesus, take me with you!*

List all of the reasons the man may have had for begging Jesus to let him go with Him (Mark 5:18).

The expression in Mark 5:18 translated "that he might be with" (or accompany, or go with) Jesus is simple enough in the original Greek text, but there may be more to it than meets the eye.

Glance back at Mark 5:3–4 and Luke 8:27. What do these verses suggest as to how long the man may have been suffering?

"For you have died, and your life is hidden with Christ in God."

—Colossians 3:3

A New Identity

While no one knows precisely how long the man suffered, Scripture certainly paints a picture of a man who had endured tremendous torment for quite some time. It reached the point where the people gave up trying to control him altogether and instead let him run naked and screaming into the night. Then, when the man was finally healed, no one came forward to claim him as family. In fact, no one seemed interested that he was healed at all. No wonder the man wanted to go with Jesus. Not only was he grateful to be rescued, but it also appeared he had nowhere else to go. The man's old life was now swallowed up in the sea, but where would he go from here?

The man's request to "be with" Jesus in Mark 5:18 may reflect a deeper desire. Whereas the man previously belonged to Satan, identified with demons and death, surely he now hoped to belong to Jesus—to be identified with *Him*. And it is here that we see the beauty of God's plan. Everything God does, He does with purpose.

Read Mark 5:19. List everything Jesus asked the man to do.

Now glance back at Mark 3:14, then complete the sentence by filling in the blanks.

> "And he appointed twelve (whom he also named apostles) so that they might be ________________ him and he might ________________ them out to ________________."

Compare and contrast Mark 3:14 with Jesus's commission to the healed man in Mark 5:19. How are they similar? What is different?

Now read Mark 3:15 and complete Jesus's expectation for His twelve disciples.

> ". . . and have authority to ________________ out demons."

Based on what we studied in Week Two, why was it important for the Twelve to receive authority to cast out demons? (Hint: glance back at page 60.)

A New Purpose

In Week Two, we explored how during Jesus's earthly ministry, He linked preaching the news of the arrival of the kingdom of God with casting out demons. Having authority over demons in the spiritual realm serves to validate the message that Jesus brings into the earthly realm. When Jesus delegates the responsibility of preaching the kingdom of God to His twelve apostles, He also bestows on them the authority of casting out demons. This was in order to demonstrate the truth of their message.

Compare Mark 3:15 with Jesus's commission in Mark 5:19. What kind of "authority" did the healed man possess that would aid in validating his message?

What does Jesus's commission in Mark 5:19 reveal about His heart for the people in that region who rejected Him?

I love this about Jesus. Though the people rejected Him, Jesus did not leave them without a witness of His grace. He did not abandon them altogether. He could have, but in His mercy, He left behind a witness to testify to His mercy and power. Jesus knew the hearts of the people were hard, but perhaps not all of them and perhaps not eternally so. The people had no realization of their own need for deliverance. After all, compared to the crazy, naked man who lived among the tombs, they surely imagined themselves to be quite dignified.

And that's the danger when we compare ourselves to others—all we have to do is find someone worse off than ourselves, and we can feel good about ourselves. One commentary author remarks, "Though we are not tortured by the devil, yet he holds us as his slaves, till the Son of God delivers us from his tyranny. Naked, torn, and disfigured, we wander about, till he restores us to soundness of mind."[17]

Until each of us recognizes that we are slaves of sin and Satan (Rom. 6:16; Eph. 2:1–2), the gift of God will have no meaning for us. But for the healed man, it was his very life! Jesus's commission to be His messenger testifies that he *does* belong—he now has a mission and a purpose: to display his new life as a witness of the Lord's mercy and power.

The man now has a mission and a purpose: to display his new life as a witness of the Lord's mercy and power.

Your Turn

"Go home to your friends [or family, or people] and tell them how much the Lord has done for you, and how he has had mercy on you" (Mark 5:19). What did Jesus equip the man with before sending him back home as His witness? Circle one.

theological training   masterful preaching   a changed life

What is the *one* most powerful asset God has equipped you with in order to be His witness?

To whom can you reach out to "tell how much the Lord has done for you, and how he has had mercy on you"? Spend some time with God in prayer, asking Him to reveal the people He is calling you to share your story with. Write a prayer of commitment as He leads you.

Day Five
Proclaiming God's Mercy

These past few weeks sure have been a wild ride! We encountered a violent windstorm, a crazed demoniac, an army of demons, and a crowd that cared more about drowning pigs than a drowning soul. But through it all was Jesus, on a rescue mission to restore *one . . . lost . . . soul.* Tearing through anything that got in His way, He refused to give up, no matter what.

As we prepare for this week's final lesson, let's do a quick review of Jesus's various encounters in Mark 5.

Glance once more at the dialogues in Mark 5:7–13 and 5:17–19. In the table, draw a line between those whom Jesus encounters in the left column and what they wanted from Jesus in the right column. Note that some of those in the left column are listed more than once.

Those Jesus Encountered	What They Wanted from Him
Townspeople begged Jesus to	not torment them before the time.
Demons begged Jesus to	not send them out of the region.
Healed man begged Jesus to	send them into the pigs.
Demons begged Jesus to	take him with Him.
Demons begged Jesus to	leave their area.

Listed below are each person or group Jesus encountered. Next to each one, circle YES or NO based on whether Jesus granted their requests.

Demons YES NO

Townspeople YES NO

Healed man YES NO

Consider the responses you circled above. Describe one or two reasons that may have factored into Jesus's decisions.

Pause to Ponder

All of us experience times when it seems that God has denied our prayers—even heartfelt ones, like the request of the healed man. What general principles from the story in Mark 5 can you apply to your own life when God does not grant your request?

Though people may recognize Jesus's power, not all embrace His presence.

Making a Choice in Light of the Miracle

The demons begged Him. The townspeople begged Him. The healed man begged Him. That's a lot of begging. And yet, while it is evident that everyone in the story recognized Jesus's power, not everyone embraced His presence. Commentator William MacDonald writes, "Jesus is seen exercising His lordship over the elements, over demons, over disease, and even over death. All these obey His word; only man refuses."[18]

When we think back on the stories we explored earlier, such as the leper in Mark 1 or the lame man in John 5, we are reminded that even when a miracle is granted, not everyone responds with a desire to follow Jesus.

Perhaps, like me, you have heard someone claim, "If God would just show Himself to me, then I would follow Him." How do the stories we have explored so far shed light on this assumption?

I Will Follow You Wherever You Go

When Jesus was preparing to leave the region, the healed man begged Jesus to take him along. Who can blame him? After being delivered from such extreme torment, I can only imagine that he would want nothing more than to cling to His Savior. Although Jesus did not grant the man's request to return with Him, He did leave him with a mission: "Go home to your friends and tell them how much the Lord has done for you, and how he has had mercy on you."

Pause to Ponder

Reflect on a time when you wanted to go in one direction, but God's will was to send you in another direction. Did you follow His plan? What were the results?

God loves us, has great compassion toward us, and came to earth to set us free. However, when God sets us free or moves us in a new direction, it is rarely solely for our own benefit. Instead, it often involves an invitation to partner with Him in His kingdom work. God has strategically gifted and placed each of us in this world to be a witness to others for the glory of His Name. With this bigger picture in mind, let's look back at the parables Jesus taught on the day He crossed the Sea of Galilee to see how those principles apply to our story.

Reread Mark 4:13–20, taking particular note of verse 20. How might this teaching have prepared the disciples for their encounter with the demoniac, especially for hearing Jesus's commission of the man in Mark 5:19?

Read Mark 5:19–20. Consider Jesus's command. How far does the man go instead? (Note: see description of the Decapolis in the margin.)

By the time Jesus left the region (Mark 5:17–18), only one person had been transformed. Considering all that Jesus battled to reach this one man—raging storms and an army of demons—what does this reveal about God's character? How does this speak to you personally?

The Decapolis, meaning "ten cities" in Greek, was originally a region of ten cities (more were added later) of largely Greek populations along the east side of Galilee and the Jordan River.

Tell of the Lord's Great Mercy

Mark 5:19–20 presents a number of interesting contrasts. Perhaps my favorite is how, in response to Jesus's command to tell the people how much *the Lord* had done for him, we read that the man proclaimed how much *Jesus* had done for him. In Jesus's day, even the Gentiles—especially those in such close proximity to the Jewish people—were aware that the Jews worshiped what they referred to as the Lord *God* Who Is the One True God. This means that the healed man may have been the first person in history to link the person of Jesus with the Lord (God) of the Old Testament.[19]

There is another subtle contrast in the passage I want to draw to your attention. When Jesus commands the man to go and *tell*, the Greek verb is *apangeilon*, which simply means to report something or bring a message. However, in verse 20, Mark writes that the man began to *proclaim* (in one translation *tell*[20]), which in Greek is a far stronger verb, *kerryssein*—the same verb Mark uses in 1:14 to describe Jesus proclaiming the arrival of the kingdom of God!

But wait, there's more! Jesus also asked the man to "go home to your friends" (literally, the command is to return home to *yours*, meaning your people), but the man didn't stop there. We read that he traveled through the Decapolis, a region likely spanning over two thousand square miles!

For the Jewish people, God's name was considered so holy that it should never be spoken out loud. So the personal name God gave to Moses concerning Himself in Exodus 3:14—I AM WHO I AM—is represented by the four Hebrew consonants YHWH, which appear as "Lord" in the Old Testament.

Considering how far he traveled, what is revealed about the man and the effect his encounter with Jesus had on him?

The man's actions are quite remarkable. Remember how the man begged Jesus to allow him to return with Him? This was not a casual request. He didn't simply ask. He *begged* Jesus. From his point of view, he likely had nowhere else to go. He may even have been afraid to return home. After all, considering the cold reception he received from the townspeople, he could only imagine how others might respond. But Jesus sees what we cannot see; He sees *behind the seen*.

For the healed man, Jesus saw what lay ahead. He saw those who would one day embrace His message. He saw the ones still in need of deliverance. And so he asked the man to return to the very place he would rather avoid. Who else would be a greater witness to reach them? Oh, the awesome and wonderful mind of God! The delivered would become a deliverer of Good News! The chained would become a champion for Christ! By his very life, the man would display the glory, power, and mercy of God!

There are no words that speak more loudly to a lost and broken world than a changed life.

The Power of a Changed Life

There are no words that speak more loudly to a lost and broken world than a changed life. For all we know, the man likely had little knowledge of the Old Testament writings, and at this point, Jesus had not yet gone to the cross. Yet none of this matters when you've been rescued from a pit so deep that hope seemed an impossible dream. Perhaps he believed that God had given up on him. That his sins were too great . . . his filthy soul too wretched for God's holy eyes. Perhaps he couldn't imagine God at all. Then one day, his Rescuer came—and nothing would ever be the same again.

When the man returned home to tell his family and friends about Jesus and all He had done for him, which do you suppose "witnessed" to the people more: What they heard or what they saw? Why?

Consider your answer to the previous question. What application does this have for you as a follower of Christ?

What about this man's story stirs your heart the most? Why?

It may be that the most beautiful part of the story is not what is written, but what is omitted. If you could ask for more details about the story, what would you ask? What else would you like to know?

I imagine there are as many answers to the last question as there are readers, but there are a few details missing in the story that stick out to me. First, I can't help but wonder what led to the man's demon possession in the first place. And how on earth did it reach the point that a *legion* of demons possessed the man? Perhaps the biggest question on many of our minds is whether the man was somehow to blame.

To me, the fact that these questions are left unanswered swells my heart with gratitude and awe at the love and mercy of God. There is no blame. No questions. No condemnation. Just *mercy*. "Go and tell them how much the Lord has done for you, and how he has had mercy on you."

Your Turn

In what ways can you identify with the mercy shown to this man? How have you experienced God's mercy?

Think of a time in your life when God fought a battle for you. In what ways did it impact your life and/or others around you? Write a prayer of thanksgiving to God for His willingness to fight for you.

Lesson Summary

What Scripture, statement, or thought was most significant to you this week? Write it down and then reword it into a prayer of response to God.

Notes

[1] C. S. Lewis, *Mere Christianity* (New York: HarperOne, 1952), 48.

[2] When the Babylonian king Nebuchadnezzar cast the prophet Daniel's three friends into a blazing furnace and they emerged unharmed, the astonished king acknowledged the three as "servants of the Most High God" and declared that "there is no other god who is able to rescue in this way" (Dan. 3:26–29). Though the king later rebelled, he ultimately acknowledged the "Most High . . . who lives forever" (Dan. 4:34).

[3] *Holman Illustrated Bible Dictionary,* ed. C. Brand et al. (Nashville: Holman Bible Publishers, 2003), s.v. "Highest," 760–61.

[4] Another reason the demons sought to speak Jesus's name may be that people in the first century considered it ominous for demons to recognize and shout out someone's name. If the demons spoke Jesus's divine name, the belief was that they would have some control over Him and perhaps hinder Him from delivering the tormented man. D. E. Garland, *Mark* (Grand Rapids, MI: Zondervan, 1996), 127–28.

[5] D. R. Acosta, "Lord of Hosts," in *The Lexham Bible Dictionary*, ed. J. D. Barry et al. (Bellingham, WA: Lexham Press, 2016).

[6] J. Calvin and W. Pringle, *Commentary on a Harmony of the Evangelists Matthew, Mark, and Luke*, vol. 1 (Bellingham, WA: Logos Bible Software, 2010), 431.

[7] Calvin and Pringle, *Commentary on a Harmony of the Evangelists*, 433.

[8] R. C. Sproul, *Mark*, 1st ed. (Orlando: Reformation Trust, 2011), 105.

[9] Bruce W. Martin, *Desperate for Hope* (Grand Rapids, MI: Revell, 2012), 57.

[10] Even here, God's mercy can be seen. Exodus 9:20–21 reveals that there was a way of escape for Pharaoh's servants who "feared the word of the Lord." Also, although many people suffered the final plague because of the king's hard heart, all who chose to join themselves to the Israelites were included under God's protection (Exod. 12:38, 48).

[11] By far the best book I've read that swells my heart, mind, and soul with absolute awe at who God is, is the little but profound book *Knowledge of the Holy*, by A. W. Tozer.

[12] Note: fear, in this context, is not referring to healthy fear as when a person is in clear, immediate danger.

[13] Calvin and Pringle, *Commentary on a Harmony of the Evangelists*, 435.

[14] William MacDonald, *Believer's Bible Commentary: Old and New Testaments*, ed. A. Farstad (Nashville: Thomas Nelson, 1995), 1399.

[15] The passage in Luke 14:25–33 is not about salvation—only the redemption through the blood of Christ can save us—but complete identification with Jesus to the degree that everything else we possess is renounced in comparison. Jesus is speaking to massive crowds who, though they followed Him around, had not committed themselves to Him. He is drawing a line in the sand: a true disciple is one who has freely abandoned everything not just to "follow" Him, but to *walk in His footsteps* and live a life fully abandoned to God.

[16] Oswald Chambers, *My Utmost for His Highest* (Grand Rapids, MI: Oswald Chambers Publications, 1986), January 11 entry.

[17] Calvin and Pringle, *Commentary on a Harmony of the Evangelists*, 436.

[18] MacDonald, *Believer's Bible Commentary*, 1398–99.

[19] Another possibility is that the man merely recognized Jesus as a man sent from God. However, given the man's firsthand experience of being possessed by a legion of demons, it is far more reasonable that he—perhaps more than anyone—knew that only God Himself was powerful enough to bring an army of demons to its knees.

[20] The NIV translates this word as "tell," and the KJV translates it as "report."

NOTES

NOTES

WEEK FIVE

EMBRACING GOD'S RESCUE

When Jesus entered the physical world roughly two thousand years ago, people were suffering from all kinds of prisons: disease, political oppression, legalism. As we discovered in Week Two, in the midst of all this suffering, there was one torment no one was able to conquer: *demons*. Yet even this is merely a shadow of the greatest prison of all. A prison that has kept the human race bound in chains from the very beginning: sin. Not "sins," but *sin*: "[T]he Scriptures declare that we are all prisoners of sin . . . . But when the right time came, God sent his Son" (Gal. 3:22a, 4:4a NLT).

Every religion aims to deal with sins, but only the true gospel of God deals with *sin*—the ultimate and first cause of all death, evil, corruption, and wickedness (Gen. 3:6–11; James 1:14–15). Two thousand years ago, Jesus came to earth on a rescue mission. To rescue not our lives, but our souls. Behind every act of mercy and every miracle Jesus performed during His earthly ministry is God's heart calling us to embrace this glorious truth—to point us to the *God Who Rescues Me*.

DAY ONE

Stepping Out of Your Comfort Zone

As we travel with Jesus through the beginning of His earthly ministry, we witness Him perform many miracles, including casting out demons with merely a word

(Mark 1:23–27, 34; see also Matt. 8:16). In every scenario, Jesus encounters the possessed person face-to-face. However, based on Mark 7:24–30 (which we will explore in the days ahead), Jesus's authority is not limited by time or space. He can just as easily cast out demons from a distance as He can when they are standing right in front of Him.

If Jesus can merely say the word and demons are cast out, why do you suppose He went to such great lengths to meet Legion face-to-face? List as many reasons as you can think of.

I love the fact that Jesus is so personal. He could just as easily have cast out the demons from the other side of the Sea of Galilee. He could have spared Himself the time and trouble of crossing the sea, battling the storms, confronting the army of demons, and enduring rejection from the townspeople—but He did not. Jesus had far more on His mind than simply setting the man free from demons.

What do you suppose was the man's *greatest* need?

The man's immediate need was rescue from the demons that tormented him; however, his greatest need of all was not to be emptied, but to be filled. Filled with the knowledge of the Living God who loved him so much that He was willing to go to great lengths to rescue one . . . lost . . . soul. For him to meet his Rescuer face-to-face, and to know the Person behind his miraculous deliverance. When Jesus sent him back home, the man's mission and message was not simply that he was set free from a legion of demons, as miraculous as his healing was. There was a far greater purpose going on *behind the seen*.

Our greatest need is not to be emptied, but to be filled. Filled with the knowledge of the Living God who went to great lengths to rescue His lost children.

What was the focus of the man's mission, according to Mark 5:19?

If Jesus had merely healed the man from a distance, how might the man's life and mission have been different?

The Means to a Glorious End

The man's story—like all testimonies of God's grace, mercy, and power—is merely the means to a glorious end. A changed life is the gift every follower of Jesus is given in order to tell others of the Living God. When Jesus commissions the man with a message of God's mercy, the man's transformed life is evidence that Jesus possesses the power and authority of God. This is important because it would not be until after Jesus rises from the dead that a more thorough understanding of who Jesus was could be grasped.

A changed life is the gift every follower of Jesus is given in order to tell others of the Living God.

Pause to Ponder

What testimony has God entrusted to you?
How has His transforming grace, power, and mercy in your life been used to draw others to Him?

If Jesus had merely cast out the legion from the opposite shore, the man would have been healed, but still lost. Still empty. Without hope. Without purpose. Had he not experienced the love of Jesus firsthand and been entrusted with a message of mercy, how tantalizing a target he would have become for the enemy once again! Other than the demons departing his body, nothing would have changed. How easy it would have been for him to stay stuck in his past, to focus only on his failures and be identified by his old life. Rather than being set free to follow Christ, he would have remained forever identified by the demons that once controlled him—helpless to break free from the shadow chains that would have still imprisoned his mind and heart. But praise God that Jesus came to do so much more! He came to personally introduce the man to the intimate love and mercy of God, to give him a new identity, a hope, and a future.

Pause to Ponder

Think of a time (or perhaps it is now) when a past sin or failure still defined you in some way. How did you (or how can you) break free from these shadow chains?

Glance back at Mark 4:13–20. How might seeing the conversion of this man, who was likely a Gentile, have:

Redefined the disciples' understanding of "good soil"? (Hint: see Mark 4:20.)

Prepared Jesus's disciples for their own commission to share the Good News in the future?

The Good News Is for All

I imagine that the conversion of the Gentile demoniac would have the disciples shaking their heads. After all, isn't the Messiah the Savior of *God's people*, the Jews? How wonderful that Jesus went to such lengths to reach this man who likely knew little, if anything, of God's commands. Without these real-life experiences, the disciples could easily have been tempted to limit their message to Jews only, or to those whom they supposed would be most receptive to the message. Yet here we see Jesus ministering not just to any Gentile, but to a man as unclean as one could imagine.

Jesus is reminding His disciples, by way of example, that the Good News is for everyone: both Jews and Gentiles (Rom. 15:9–12), as well as the outcast, the broken, and the unclean. After all, if a naked, crazed Gentile demoniac can be transformed into a messenger of God's grace, is anyone outside of God's reach? Praise God for His great mercy!

"Surely the arm of the LORD is not too short to save . . ."
—Isaiah 59:1 NIV

Pause to Ponder

How about you? Is there someone in your life you tend to view as being outside of God's reach? In what ways does the story of Legion cast doubt on this assumption?

God Promises a Hope and a Future

When we consider all that the man with the legion had endured and all the people who witnessed his tragic life, who better to deliver such a message in that region than the one who had been delivered from such torment? After all, his message is not just about what he had been delivered *from*, but more importantly, it's about the ultimate promises his deliverance points people *to*.

Perhaps no other passage portrays these promises more beautifully than John 14. It is here that Jesus reminds His followers of His promise regarding what would happen after He is crucified and raised from the dead. Let's take a look.

Read the excerpt from John 14 printed below. (Optional: read all of John 14:1–31 in your Bible). Underneath, I have listed various realities of the demoniac's life prior to his encounter with Jesus. Next to each one, fill in the blank with a word or phrase from John 14 that captures a promise addressing the man's needs. I completed the first one to get you started.

> In my Father's house are many rooms. . . . And if I go and prepare a place for you, I will come again and will take you to myself, that where I am you may be also. . . . And I will ask the Father, and he will give you another Helper [the Holy Spirit], to be with you forever . . . . I will not leave you as orphans; I will come to you. . . . Peace I leave with you; my peace I give to you. (John 14:2–3, 16, 18, 27)

Reality before Jesus	Promised to Those Who Follow Jesus
Homeless	Jesus is preparing a place for us in His *Father's house*.
Possessed by a legion of demons	The Father gives us His ____________.
Abandoned and alone	Jesus does not leave us as ____________.
Tormented in mind, body, and spirit	Jesus gives us His ____________.

Ponder the promises listed. Which one stirs your heart the most? Why?

"For I know the plans I have for you, declares the LORD, plans for welfare and not for evil, to give you a future and a hope."

—Jeremiah 29:11

For every follower of Jesus, each promise in John 14 is a precious gift. For the demoniac Jesus rescued, each one is a miracle beyond anything the man could have dreamed. Before Jesus came to him, the man was possessed by a legion of demons. Soon, the very Holy Spirit of God would fill him. Before Jesus entered his life, he was homeless and living among dead men's tombs, but Jesus promises a heavenly home in His Father's house to all who follow Him. Before Jesus came, the man was abandoned and alone—cast out from society—but after Jesus came to him, he would never be an "orphan" again. And before Jesus breathed His healing power over him, he was a deeply tormented man, running wild, screaming, naked, and bleeding, but now the very peace of Jesus would calm and heal his wounded heart.

The same peace that enabled Jesus to sleep through a raging storm would take residence in this man's soul and carry him far beyond what he could have asked or imagined. This is the hope for all who are in Christ: though absent from Christ's physical presence, we are never alone. Jesus did not grant the man's request to return with Him because He had a greater purpose in mind: "Go home to your friends and tell them how much the Lord has done for you, and how he has had mercy on you." It is as if Jesus is saying, *I want you to go home and prepare hearts in this region because I am coming back; and as you go, this I promise—you do not go alone*. "And he went away and began to proclaim in the Decapolis how much Jesus had done for him, and everyone marveled" (Mark 5:20).

This is the hope for all who are in Christ: though absent from Christ's physical presence, we are never alone.

Your Turn

Earlier in today's lesson, I asked you to ponder if there is someone in your life whom you tend to view as being outside of God's reach. Or perhaps there is someone you do not regard as out of God's reach, but the relationship has wearied you and you are tempted to give up. Take a moment to ask God if He has placed this person in your life for a reason. How might God be calling you to minister or be a witness to this person? Perhaps through prayer, friendship, acts of service? Write a prayer of commitment as God leads you.

How else may God be calling you to surrender your agenda or step out of your comfort zone to do something new for His glory? What would it look like to accept His assignment?

Day Two
Tearing Down the Prison Walls

At the end of yesterday's lesson, we saw the healed demoniac embrace his God-given mission to proclaim the Lord's mercy and power as demonstrated by his deliverance from a legion of demons. Meanwhile, Jesus, having completed His own mission to heal the tormented man, crossed back over to the other side of the lake. And in case His disciples were tempted to dismiss the dramatic rescue of the demoniac as an isolated incident of God's mercy toward the outcast and unclean, they were about to witness yet another powerful lesson. Just as they had left a crowd behind when they crossed over (Mark 4:36), they found another crowd waiting upon their return. Little did they know that pushing their way through the sea of people were one man and one woman—each desperate for a miracle.

Read all of Mark 5:21–34 two times through; if possible, read it once out loud. Briefly describe the events in your own words.

What stood out to you the most in the passage? Why?

Clean versus Unclean

At first, it may seem odd that these two stories are sandwiched together; but nothing in Scripture is random. By placing these stories immediately after the healing of the man with the legion, and then layering them one inside the other, the author draws our attention to the fact that a relationship exists between them. To draw this out further, we will first explore some of the contrasts in the text between the synagogue ruler whose daughter is ill and the woman who suffers from continuous menstrual hemorrhaging.

In Jesus's day, synagogue rulers were typically wealthy and highly respected, and they most certainly endeavored to keep themselves ceremonially clean according to Jewish laws. In contrast, according to Old Testament law, the woman would have been considered thoroughly unclean—even untouchable!—for all of her twelve years of suffering (see Lev. 15:19, 25). Being unclean also meant that the woman would have been prohibited from entering the temple in order to participate in the religious ceremonies and community gatherings.

Try to imagine what this woman's life would have been like. Describe all the ways she would have been suffering.

What aspect of this woman's suffering seems most tragic to you personally? Why?

According to Jewish law, the mere touch of this woman would have defiled the person she touched. And yet, in her actions we see evidence that there was something in the woman's faith that drew her to Jesus. Something that convinced her that to touch Jesus would not defile Him, but in fact would set her free from her defiling disease.

Pause to Ponder

Think of a time when you hesitated to approach God, perhaps feeling too unclean or unworthy. How did you overcome your fears?

Whether the woman was driven by a hidden, inner belief or the invisible pull of the Holy Spirit, her daring touch reveals a faith in which Jesus is somehow above and beyond such laws.[1] Perhaps that is why God orchestrated her entry into the divine story precisely where it would dramatically intersect—even disrupt—the story of the man whose daughter was dying. After all, as a synagogue ruler, it was this man's job to serve as strict guardian of the Jewish law.

In the chart, I have listed several traits typical of a synagogue ruler as well as additional details from the story in Mark 5:21–34. In the right-hand column, identify the contrasting realities that pertain to the woman. If you notice additional contrasts, list those as well. I completed two to get you started.

Synagogue Ruler	Suffering Woman
Ceremonially clean	*Unclean*
Wealthy	*Poor (spent all she had on physicians)*
Named (Jairus)	

Man	
Approached Jesus boldly	
Spoke to Jesus	
Other	

Stepping Out in Faith

The physical suffering of the woman would have been awful enough, but I can only imagine how the torment of being unclean and separated from community life for all those years would have left her feeling isolated and sorrowful. Except for myriad physicians, motivated by sincerity or greed or perhaps a little of both, she would likely have been shunned by all of those around her, even her family. Whereas the daughter of the synagogue ruler had a highly regarded, loving father pleading for her, this woman had no one to intercede on her behalf. She therefore braved the crowd and, as stealthily as possible, reached out to Jesus herself. And here is where we discover another wonderful reason that these two stories are placed together. To see it clearly, we will need to outline the story in its grammatical structure.

Glance once again at Mark 5:22-34. Record any parallels you can discover by identifying repeated key words, phrases, or concepts.

In Week One, we discussed a literary pattern called chiastic structure (or chiasm). It can be recognized by an intersection in a passage of mirror words, concepts, or events, which are used to draw the reader's attention to a key point or climactic event that the author wants to emphasize. In the stories shared in Mark 5:22–34, there is added complexity in verses 25–27, in which the author inserts a series of seven participles between introducing the woman and conveying her first primary action.

When we outline the structure and set aside the lengthy series of participles[2] that describe the woman and what led her into the scene, the chiasm becomes clearer. Therefore, to help us see the chiastic structure more easily in the visual exercise that follows, I have omitted the participles from the outline. In order to identify parallel words, phrases, or concepts, pairs of letters (A with A′, B with B′, and so on) will be used.

In the chiasm outlined below, fill in the missing words or phrases based on the events in Mark 5:22–34. (Note: Bible versions that adhere to a more literal translation, such as ESV, NASB, or NKJV, are best suited for this exercise.)

A The synagogue ruler:
Saw Jesus and fell at His _________.
He implored Jesus that his _________ was dying.
He asked Jesus to come so that she would be *made well.*
B A woman in the crowd _________ His garment.
C She believed by *touching* the _________, she would be made well.
D She felt in her body she was _________ of her disease.
D[1] Jesus perceived _________ went out from Him.
C[1] Jesus asked, "Who _________ my *garments*?"
B[1] "You see the _________ . . . yet you say, 'Who *touched* me?'"
A[1] The woman:
Fell at Jesus's *feet.*
Jesus called her "_________."
Jesus declared that her faith had *made her well.*

Stepping into the Light

Picture the scene. The woman does not know exactly who Jesus is, but her heart compels her toward Him. She does not know what consequences she will face for daring to touch this great Healer from God, but she reaches out her hand. Tearing through the crowd and every cultural and religious barrier, she does the one thing the law forbids her to do—and immediately the flow of blood ceases.

Suddenly, Jesus turns around, demanding to know who touched Him. She knows she is exposed. When she can no longer hide behind her veil, or fear, or shame, she comes forward, falls at His feet, and confesses everything. Silence washes over the crowd. All eyes are fixed on her. Those nearest quickly move away. Some are indignant—maybe even disgusted. Perhaps one or two have pity. Slowly, she looks up into the eyes of Love, as tender mercy floods her thirsty soul.

Pause to Ponder

Try to imagine yourself in this woman's sandals. What part of Jesus's response speaks to your heart the most? Why?

I love that the first word Jesus speaks over her is *daughter*. This was likely the first time in at least twelve years anyone had spoken words of affection over her—and not only of affection, but of acceptance. She is the only person in Scripture Jesus personally calls daughter.[3] This is the beautiful reason her story collides with the daughter who is dying.

Daughter, your faith has made you well; go in peace, and be healed of your disease.

There is so much packed into Jesus's simple words. After Jesus wraps the woman's lonely soul in His Spirit's embrace by calling her daughter, He then comforts her with two precious assurances. At a glance, the phrases "made well" and "healed" may seem similar, but the words in Mark 5:34 are quite different in Greek. "Made well" is translated from one Greek word, *sozo*, which means to save, rescue, or deliver. It is the same word the synagogue ruler uses when he begs Jesus to come save his daughter from death. It is also used throughout the New Testament concerning *eternal* salvation! In other words, Jesus's words can easily be translated as "Your faith has saved you." What a precious promise!

But Jesus is not finished. He then adds, "[G]o in peace, and be healed of your disease." Although Jesus came to rescue our souls from a fate worse than death, He also knows firsthand the pain and trials of our daily lives. The verb in the second half of verse 34 is *hygies* in Greek, which relates to physical health. You probably recognize the word as the basis of the English word "hygiene." The Greek word simply means to heal or cure. Nevertheless, while her physical healing is a blessing indeed, the greatest gift is salvation through faith in Jesus.

Tearing Down the Walls

Glance back at Mark 5:27-31, which reveals the climax of the story. How many times does the verb "touch" appear in the text? __________ Do you think this is significant? Why or why not?

Read Leviticus 15:19-25. How many times do the following words appear in the text?

touch (or touches) _______ unclean (or uncleanness) _______

Contrast the seriousness of this woman's failure to adhere to the law with her daring determination to touch Jesus. What conclusions can you draw?

Why do you suppose Jesus honored the woman's willingness to disregard[4] the Old Testament laws in order to reach Him?

Read Matthew 5:17 and Galatians 3:23-26. How do these verses shed light on Jesus's response to the woman's actions?

"So in Christ Jesus you are all children of God through faith." —Galatians 3:26 NIV

In the story of the bleeding woman, not only is the verb "touch" repeated four times in the text, but every occurrence surrounds the climactic point of the story. After suffering for twelve years, having lost everything and desperate for a miracle, the unclean reaches out to touch the Holy One. Tearing through the barriers of the crowd, the shame, the pain, *and the law*, the woman finally breaks free from her prison . . . and Jesus is delighted by her faith.

I Am Clean — *a poem I wrote*

You cleanse my heart, oh King—
by your blood I am made clean.

So what is that echo there—
—whispering my sin?
What is that shadow there—
—lurking within?

You are crowned with glory—
none can compare.
So why is shame
waiting for me there?

Lies! Lies from the enemy—
of a time long ago.
Forgotten by You—
on a Cross far away.

Cleanse me, oh Lord, of my shame and sin.
Remind me, oh Lord, that You are still within.

Your Turn

Throughout each of our lives, we will find ourselves in various prisons, whether built by others or manufactured in our own minds.

What barriers have you had to break through in your life in order to reach Jesus or to strengthen or nurture your walk with God? What were the results?

Is there something right now that has a stronghold on you? If so, what do you need to ask from God? What would it look like for you to reach out to Jesus in faith in this matter?

Day Three

Recognizing Our Need for a Savior

Yesterday, we explored the two intertwined stories that immediately follow the account of Legion. But we still don't know what happened to the little girl. Let's find out.

Read Mark 5:35–43. Then answer the questions that follow.

When the ruler is told that his daughter is dead, what does Jesus say to him? Rewrite Jesus's words as they appear in the text.

Contrast the ruler's initial boldness with the fear he is now experiencing. How can you relate to his struggle?

Read Numbers 19:11, 22. According to this law, what would be said of Jesus based on His actions in Mark 5:41?

Jesus touches the lepers, casts out demons, declares the outcast a daughter, and even reaches out to grasp the hand of a dead child. He is the only One who, rather than becoming defiled, makes others clean with just His touch—or even a word. Just as Jesus declared Himself "lord of the Sabbath," and demonstrated His rule over creation by calming the seas, here we see that He can even make the unclean clean. Wherever He went, Jesus set people free from their prisons: whether it was demons, legalism, disease, or even death. And yet, all of these serve as merely a foreshadowing for His greatest deliverance of all.

Reaching Out for Help

In Scripture, we can often gain rich insights by studying where in the text a story is placed. Yesterday, we explored two miraculous healings that immediately followed the story of Jesus delivering the man with the legion. When we step back to gain an even wider view, as well as take into account additional events recorded by the other Gospel writers, we find that the account of the demon-possessed man is situated among quite a number of miraculous encounters all sharing one thing in common.

In the table below, I have identified a number of events in chronological order. Next to each Scripture reference, answer the questions in the other columns based on the text. I completed several for you.

Scripture	Who was ill or suffering?	Who approached Jesus for help?
Mark 2:1–5 (this story is a review)	*A paralyzed man*	*Four friends who carried the man*
Matthew 8:5–13		
Mark 5:21–24		
Mark 5:25–28		
Mark 6:53–56	*Various sick people*	*Friends/family [implied] of the sick*
Mark 7:24–30	*A Gentile woman's little daughter*	*The child's mother*
Mark 7:31–35		
Mark 8:22–25	*A blind man*	*People who knew the man*

Note the variety of intercessors coming to Jesus: a group of companions carrying their paralyzed friend, a Roman soldier interceding for his servant, a father pleading for his young daughter, and a woman so desperate for a cure that she reaches out to Jesus herself.

In the case of the man possessed with the legion, who came to Jesus interceding on his behalf? What does this aspect of the story reveal about God's character, and how does this speak to you personally?

This is one of the reasons I am personally moved by this story. The people in each of the other scenarios all had one thing in common: they recognized their need or that of a loved one, and they reached out to Jesus for help. However, when neither the demoniac nor anyone else came to Jesus on his behalf, Jesus Himself battled the raging sea and confronted a legion of demons to rescue this one broken man.

In Need of Rescue

At one time or another, all of us find ourselves in need of someone's help. When I was thirteen years old, I was at a summer camp in upstate New York. My favorite activity was singing songs around a campfire (even though I can't sing). One evening, a few of the counselors decided to take a group of us campers for a walk around the other side of the lake. Because the air was warm and the water splashing along the sandy bank was so refreshing, several of us took off our shoes to walk along the edge of the water.

Moments later, I cried out in pain, crumpling to the ground after stepping on a large piece of glass, which was buried in the sand. The counselors came running toward me. One of the male counselors quickly lifted me on to his back, wrapping his arms behind my knees, and raced back to camp. When we arrived at the medical station, the nurse immediately set out to clean and bandage my wounded foot. I spent the rest of the week on crutches, but thankfully, no permanent damage was done.

Each of us will face times when we know we need help but are powerless to do anything about it. If this is true in the physical realm, how much more powerless are we when we fall in the spiritual realm? Who will come to our rescue and carry us safely home?

"No one can come to me unless the Father who sent me draws him."
—Jesus (John 6:44a)

Read John 6:44a in the margin. Rewrite this truth in your own words as if you were explaining it to a friend who had only a vague understanding of the Christian faith.

Our Greatest Need

Throughout the Gospel accounts, the stories of people coming to Jesus and being healed of disease or demons served to validate His message and identity, as well as to foreshadow a greater deliverance to come. In each of the events surrounding the story of the man delivered from a legion of demons, someone came to Jesus seeking help. However, when it comes to humanity being delivered from our greatest affliction of all—sin—we are actually far more like the man with the legion. Helpless. Hopeless. Without anyone pleading on our behalf. Without the ability, or even the awareness, to seek rescue ourselves.

Scripture plainly teaches that no one seeks God (Ps. 14:2–3; see also Ps. 53:2–3 and Rom. 3:10–11). Apart from God's grace working in our hearts, none of us is drawn to the love of Christ. It is only when we are sharply confronted with the reality of our sin and our offense to a holy God that we will either walk toward the light in repentance or recoil from it in hatred (John 3:19–21). Even then, our faith to step into the light is a gracious gift from God (Eph. 2:8–9).

Apart from God's grace working in our hearts, none of us is drawn to the love of Christ.

Pause to Ponder

How would you describe the gospel message to a friend in two to three sentences?

In the space below, write Jesus's words as recorded in Mark 1:15, which mark the beginning of Jesus's ministry.

Now read Mark 3:14–15 and 6:7, 12–13, where Jesus appoints, then sends, His twelve apostles (meaning "sent ones"). What message are they to proclaim, according to Mark 6:12?

What was the purpose of giving them authority to heal and cast out demons? (Hint: we explored this in Day Two of Week Two.)

Compare and contrast Jesus's message in Mark 1:15 with the description of the gospel message you shared in the previous Pause to Ponder section.

The purpose of giving the disciples power to heal and cast out demons was simple: to validate their message. In one sense, the message has not changed. From Old Testament prophets to John the Baptist, Jesus, the apostles, and the book of Revelation, the message to humanity has been simple: repent. In fact, the book of Revelation begins by urging the churches to repent (chapters 2 and 3) and then proceeds to pronounce judgment on humanity "because they did not repent" (Rev. 9:20–21, 16:9–11).

However, Jesus's message included something new: the kingdom of God is near. Soon Jesus would be revealed as Israel's Messiah and, as the disciples proclaimed *this* truth, their message would be validated by their power to heal and cast out demons.

When it comes to sharing the gospel with unbelievers, how does the Bible's message of repentance compare with what you typically hear preached today?

Now read Romans 5:6, 8–10, which is printed below. Note anything interesting that stands out to you in the text.

> For while we were still weak [i.e., morally], at the right time Christ died for the ungodly. . . . [B]ut God shows his love for us in that while we were still sinners, Christ died for us. Since, therefore, we have now been justified by his blood, much more shall we be saved by him from the wrath of God. For if while we were enemies we were reconciled to God by the death of his Son, much more, now that we are reconciled, shall we be saved by his life.

Next, fill in the blanks based on the text you just read. I completed a few for you.

While we were still *weak*, Christ ________ for the *ungodly*.

While we were still ________, Christ ________ for ________.

While we were ____________, we were reconciled to God by the ________ of his ________.

Take a few moments to ponder the previous three statements. What observations can you make?

Before any of us can repent and ask Jesus to save us from our sin, we must recognize that, because of our rebellion and sin, we are all enemies of God.

At a glance, it may seem as if the apostle Paul is merely restating the same thing in different ways, but did you notice the progression of descriptors he uses of his readers? Scripture does not merely state that we are weak (as in morally weak), or even that we are sinners, but that, apart from the blood of Christ, we—just like the legion of demons—are enemies of God. For some, that may seem a hard truth to swallow. The reality is that before any of us can repent and ask Jesus to save us, we must recognize that because of our rebellion and sin, we are all enemies of God. Cleansing us from our sin cost God the blood of His own Son.

Your Turn

Have you ever considered yourself an *enemy* of God? Why or why not?

You and I live in a world suffering under the weight of sin, and there is only One who can save us. Have you repented of your sin and embraced Jesus Christ as your personal Lord and Savior? If not, what may be standing in the way?

Day Four

Announcing the Coming King

"The reason the Son of God appeared was to destroy the works of the devil" (1 John 3:8b). We began this week's lesson with the precious reminder that Jesus came

to earth on a rescue mission. Every miraculous story of deliverance—from the demon-possessed people in the synagogue to the lepers, to the paralytic, to the centurion's servant, to the man with the legion, to the synagogue ruler's daughter, to the bleeding woman and so many others—points to this precious truth: that Jesus is the Messiah, our Deliverer and King.

From the beginning, God in His mercy promised a Savior who would conquer Satan, sin, and death: "I will put enmity between you and the woman, and between your offspring and her offspring; he shall bruise your head, and you shall bruise his heel" (Gen. 3:15).

Read 1 John 3:8b, which is quoted at the beginning of this lesson, and Hebrews 2:14–15 in your Bible. Then answer the questions that follow.

List everything Christ accomplished, according to these verses.

Of the list you made, which one speaks to your heart the most? Why?

What might the phrase regarding Satan (or the devil) having "power over death" mean? (Hint: see Rom. 6:16, 23.)

It is important to remember that, as we studied in the story of Job in Week Two, Satan's power is not absolute; it is under the complete control of God, the Sovereign Ruler over the universe, which includes life and death.[5] Satan's "power over death" relates to his *enslavement* of people to sin (which leads to death; Rom. 6:16), and, as the adversary,[6] his legitimate *accusations* that they deserve death (Rom. 6:23). Nothing more.

In Hebrews 2:14, the word translated "power" is *kratos* in Greek, which relates to dominion. It is the same word found in 1 Peter 4:11, which promises that to Jesus alone belongs the "glory and dominion forever and ever."[7] Therefore, to keep these passages in perspective, we must recognize that the emphasis in 1 John 3:8 and Hebrews 2:14 is not on Satan's power but on *Christ's* triumph over Satan, sin, and death through the cross.[8] This is the victory God promised Adam and Eve in that first garden paradise so many centuries ago. Although they tragically forfeited their delegated authority over the earth to Satan, who is currently the "ruler of this world" (John 12:31–33), his time is short. A new King is coming!

SUPPLEMENTAL READING

WHAT DOES IT MEAN THAT SATAN IS RULER OF THIS WORLD?

After Jesus was baptized and then led into the desert to be tempted by the devil, He never challenged Satan's right to offer Him the kingdoms of the world, but only the means by which Jesus would reclaim possession of them.[9] Satan became ruler of this world (John 12:31) when Adam and Eve forfeited their authority over to him in the Garden. Authors Dean and Ice write, "By declaring their independence against God, Adam and Eve became citizens of Satan's kingdom and . . . [t]he world and the human race became legally under Satan's authority."[10]

The same adversary who was at work then is just as active in our world today. We live in a world plagued by evil because Satan is the one who sets the agenda. "The whole world lies in the power of the evil one" (1 John 5:19). However, while Satan currently enjoys "a certain freedom of operation, within divinely appointed limits, to act as God's opponent during the present age,"[11] his days are numbered. The entire Bible centers on God's plan to reclaim His kingdom and His sovereign authority over the earth, which will happen at the end of time (which, I would argue, is sooner than we may think.)

Until then, you and I must live between two realms: the earth where Satan reigns and heaven, our true home (Phil. 3:20). As citizens of heaven, it is vital that we remember, just as in the Garden of Eden, Satan cannot *make* people sin. Rather, because every human being after Adam and Eve has been born polluted with sin, all Satan has to do is present the opportunity. In fact, James 1:14 reminds us that he doesn't even need to do that. The reality is that apart from Christ, we are all slaves to sin (Rom. 6:16).

Because God's Holy Spirit lives within us, we can actually choose *not* to sin.

But there is good news! Those who are in Christ have been "born again." We have been given a new heart and new spirit. Because God's Holy Spirit lives within us, Scripture teaches that we can actually choose *not* to sin (Rom. 6:6; 1 John 3:9 and 5:18). Granted, there are times we still fail (Rom. 7:23); but if we are abiding in Christ, we are growing stronger every day. And praise God that when we do fail, "If we confess our sins, he is faithful and just to forgive us our sins and to cleanse us from all unrighteousness" (1 John 1:9).

Yet those who reject God's gift of salvation can never point to their sin and claim, "the devil made me do it." The book of Revelation records that during Jesus's thousand-year[12] earthly reign, people who survive God's righteous judgments will live on an earth free from Satan's influence. And yet, no sooner is Satan released from his prison, than many unite themselves to him in a vain attempt to overthrow Christ's authority (Rev. 20:7–9). All along, their rebellion had been simmering beneath the surface, *apart from any demonic activity.* As soon as the opportunity presents itself, their rebellion is unleashed in full fury.

The reality is that although Satan is the "ruler of this world," in the end, all people will realize that their greatest enemy was not Satan, but their own selves and the sin to which they were enslaved. For some, it will mean eternal damnation "because they refused to love the truth and so be saved" (2 Thess. 2:10; see also John 3:19 and Rom. 2:8). But those who love God will rejoice because Jesus has defeated the enemy: not just Satan and the grave, but sin itself! By His blood, He has made it possible for all who come to Him to be forgiven and delivered from the domain of darkness and transferred into the kingdom of God's Son (Col. 1:13). Praise His Name!

"He has delivered us from the domain of darkness and transferred us to the kingdom of his beloved Son." —Colossians 1:13

The King Is Coming!

Satan's time is short; a new King is coming! In fact, you may find that after today's lesson, your perception of the events surrounding Jesus's arrival on earth have taken on a whole new dimension. . . . Perhaps you are familiar with the story of Jesus entering Jerusalem riding on a donkey, the Triumphal Entry, as scholars call it. The event fulfilled the prophecy in Zechariah 9:9, whereby Israel's king would enter Jerusalem, "righteous and having salvation . . . humble and mounted on a donkey." However, before we explore our King's triumphal entry into Jerusalem, let's step back and gaze upon the triumphal entry of His miraculous birth with fresh eyes to see how it sheds light on our story of Legion.

For untold generations, reading Luke's Gospel account of the birth of Christ has been a treasured Christmas tradition, as well as serving as the backdrop of innumerable children's Christmas productions. However, after we look at a few passages more closely, you may discover that you never look at another Christmas production the same way again!

Read Luke 2:8-14 (Optional: read Luke 1:26-35 and 2:1-21).

Luke's Gospel provides the most detail surrounding Christ's birth, and it is the only Gospel to mention the shepherds guarding their sheep in the fields outside Bethlehem. In fact, many of these sheep would likely be used as sacrifices to God.

It is no coincidence that God chooses to send His heavenly host to announce the newborn King to a band of sleepy shepherds. At a time when the surrounding pagan nations were offering filthy sacrifices to idols, demons, and ancestors, Jesus

"The LORD of hosts is mustering a host for battle. They come from a distant land, from the end of the heavens."

—Isaiah 13:4-5

came into the world to be the One true sacrifice: "the Lamb of God who takes away the sin of the world." But there is even more going on here than meets the eye.

Glance again at Luke 2:8–14. Now read Isaiah 13:4–5 in the margin, which represents merely one occurrence among nearly 250 references to God as the "Lord of hosts" in the Old Testament. Finally, write Luke 2:13 in the space below.

When you read or hear the term "angelic [or heavenly] host," what comes to mind? How do you picture it?

In the Old Testament, the vast majority of the references to God as Lord of hosts coincide with matters relating to war, power, strength, God subduing His enemies, or the Israelites seeking refuge in God from their enemies. As we studied briefly last week: God has an army. And in case anyone was in doubt, Joshua 5:14 introduces an imposing stranger (who is likely the preincarnate Christ[13]) with a drawn sword who declares plainly, "I am the commander of the army of the LORD." The word translated "army" in Joshua 5:14 is *tsaba* in Hebrew. It is the identical word translated "host" in describing God as the Lord of hosts throughout the Old Testament. Wherever Scripture uses the title Lord of hosts, the reader is expected to visualize God with a powerful army.[14] The *New Living Translation* helps capture the feel of the text by translating this title as "LORD of Heaven's Armies."

Try to imagine life as an Israelite in Old Testament times, when ruthless nations with mighty armies threaten you and your loved ones on every side. What difference would it make to believe that *your* God is the Lord of Heaven's Armies?

How about in your own life right now? What difference would it make to believe that *your* God is the Lord of Heaven's Armies?

In Luke 2:13, the word commonly translated "host" is *stratias* in Greek, which literally means *army*. (The same root word occurs in Revelation 19:14 in reference to "the armies of heaven.") This, along with the numerous Old Testament references to God as "Lord of hosts," means that when Luke describes "a multitude of the heavenly host" announcing Jesus's birth, he expects his readers to envision an angelic army!

Do you think this is significant? Why or why not?

In what ways does the concept of a military presence at Christ's birth compare with the story of Legion?

How does this military presence enhance your understanding of the events surrounding Christ's birth?

Thankfully, rather than coming to declare war, the angelic army in Luke's gospel came to praise God and deliver a message of peace. To announce the arrival of the Christ (that is: the King), who was also Savior and Lord. His birth signaled the glorious promise of a new kingdom where peace will reign forevermore.

Pause to Ponder

How often, on average, do you ponder God's promise of a future kingdom where righteousness, peace, and justice will reign? Circle one.

daily weekly monthly rarely never

If you circled rarely or never, how might your prayer life change if you incorporated more time meditating on Christ's return and the coming kingdom of God?

What do you look forward to the most when King Jesus returns to physically set up His kingdom on earth?

"I have set my King on Zion, my holy hill." —Psalm 2:6

I don't know about you, but there are many things I am looking forward to when Christ returns to "make all things new" (Rev. 21:1–5): the end of wars and hatred, the freedom from fears, the joy of relationships void of pretense, gazing upon the beauty of God's uncorrupted new creation, and so much more. However, what I desire most of all is the day I will see Jesus face-to-face, the day I will look into His eyes and see His holy love—and have no impulse to run away and hide in fear or shame. Throughout my life, I have peered into eyes of hatred, of anger, of lust. . . . Oh, how I long to gaze into the eyes of Love! To live in a world ruled by a king who loves His people with a pure, unconditional love. To live in a kingdom where righteousness reigns forever.

A Promise of Peace

In biblical times, if a king entered a region on horseback with his army, it signaled that he had come to make war. If the king entered on a donkey with his army, it announced that he had come bringing peace. When we consider Jesus's triumphal entry into Jerusalem after the heavenly army's announcement at His birth, we begin to see how the events all tie together.

Nevertheless, when a king arrived in a region bringing peace, it did not mean that the new king would not make changes. Every king had a vision of how his kingdom would be ruled, and Jesus was no exception. After His triumphal entry into Jerusalem, Jesus's first order of business was to cleanse God's holy temple. The priesthood had become corrupt. When Jesus overthrew the moneychangers in the temple, the chief priests had finally had enough. They now plotted to get rid of Him (Mark 11:18). When Judas, one of Jesus's disciples, agreed to betray Jesus, they finally got their chance.

Your Turn

In Day One of Week Four, I asked you to spend some time meditating on one or two titles and attributes of God that you have not pondered lately. Go back to the end of Day One in Week Four and share any insights you gained or what impact it had on your prayer times.

How can you take comfort in knowing that to King Jesus alone belongs the "glory and dominion forever and ever"? What does this mean for you as you live your days in a world still suffering under sin?

Day Five
Witnessing God's Greatest Gift

I don't know when my coworker started to despise me. I don't even know why. I began to sense something was different months before, but her change of attitude was so subtle, I wasn't sure if I was imagining it. Several times, I thought about asking her if I had done something to offend her, but I feared she would become defensive and I would make the situation worse. I suppose now I'll never know if I made the right decision. She gave notice a few weeks ago that she would be retiring—something she had been looking forward to. I took the opportunity to chat with another coworker about planning some kind of celebration. "Perhaps we could all take her out to lunch," I suggested.

A few days later, a number of coworkers gathered near our offices around lunchtime. It didn't take me long to realize that a celebration lunch had been planned; in fact, it was planned long before—and I was not invited. One of my other coworkers looked confused when he saw I was not joining them. It was awkward and painful. Truth be told: I was hurt. I didn't know how I would make it through the day.

That afternoon, when my coworker snapped at me for asking a question, her unexpected outburst pierced the still-tender wound. No one was nearby to witness the exchange—no one except the Spirit of God; nothing escapes His notice. Quickly, I made my way to the restroom. Thankfully, it was deserted as I hid myself, silently pouring my hurt out to God. I was hurt but also frustrated that I had actually succumbed to tears. It seemed that the thick skin I had built up in years past had softened. I suppose that's a good thing; God doesn't want our hearts to be calloused.

"And I will give you a new heart, and a new spirit I will put within you. And I will remove the heart of stone from your flesh and give you a heart of flesh."

—Ezekiel 36:26

Pause to Ponder

Think of a time when you were unjustly treated, felt despised, or were rejected. How did you respond? What did you learn or how did God change you through the experience?

The next morning during my prayer time, I knew I had to pray for my coworker, if for no other reason than to guard myself against anger and bitterness—against reerecting stone walls in my heart. Walls that Christ's love had paid a high price to tear down. As I began praying for her, my heart softened as I remembered all

too well how broken I had been apart from the love of God. *How many people did I hurt over the years without even realizing it,* I wondered to myself. I chose to write her a kind note apologizing for frustrating her. As I did so, I marveled at how much God had changed my heart over the years. Truly, my strength and desire to respond this way came solely from God (Phil. 2:13–15). His Spirit within me helped me decide that it made no difference who was in the wrong: only that the Name of the One to whom I belong is honored. When I arrived at work that morning, I left the note at my coworker's desk. Though my efforts were never acknowledged, my heart was at peace.

Jesus never asks us to walk a road that He Himself did not already pave before us.

Scripture assures us that as followers of Christ, the world will hate us for no other reason than that we belong to Him. "If the world hates you, know that it has hated me before it hated you. If you were of the world, the world would love you as its own; but because you are not of the world, but I chose you out of the world, therefore the world hates you" (John 15:18–19; see also verses 20–21). Jesus never asks us to walk a road that He Himself did not already pave before us.

Despised and Rejected

For as long as God's beloved people of Israel could remember, they looked forward to their promised king, the Messiah. Yet, in describing the Messiah, the prophet Isaiah writes, "He was despised and rejected by men, a man of sorrows and acquainted with grief. . . . By oppression and judgment he was taken away" (Isa. 53:3, 8).

"No one takes it from me, but I lay it down of my own accord. I have authority to lay it down, and I have authority to take it up again." —John 10:18

Read Mark 14:43–46 and Matthew 26:53. What does the fact that Jesus could prevent His arrest (whether with a heavenly army or by any other means) reveal about His control over the events? (Hint: see also John 10:18 in the margin.)

Perhaps you have heard it said that the God in the Old Testament is a God of wrath, whereas the God in the New Testament, as reflected in the life of Jesus, is a God of grace. What danger may lurk behind this line of thinking?

God Never Changes

God never changes. If He did, we could never count on a single attribute of His nature, whether it be mercy, justice, love, faithfulness, kindness, or anything else, because it could change in a moment. From the beginning, God has shown Himself merciful and full of grace: in the Garden of Eden when He clothed Adam and Eve to cover their shame; in the period of Israel's kings when, for example, God spared King David when his sins of adultery and murder deserved death; in the New Testament when Jesus likewise spared a woman caught in adultery.

He has also shown Himself as a holy king to be feared, exacting punishment on His enemies: in condemnation against His ungodly priests and rebellious nation; in judgment of the world's sin on the cross; in the frightening wrath to come on humanity for rejecting His mercy and grace (Rev. 6–19).[15] God is merciful and loving, holy and just. To elevate one aspect of God's character over another is to make a god of our own design, which is idolatry—the very first offense God commanded we guard against.

"The LORD is merciful and gracious, slow to anger and abounding in steadfast love. . . . [A]s far as the east is from the west, so far does he remove our transgressions from us."

—Psalm 103:8, 12

PAUSE TO PONDER

When you meditate on God and who He is, how can you guard yourself from overemphasizing one aspect of His character over another? Why is this important?

"Are You the Christ?"

After Jesus is arrested in the garden of Gethsemane, He is brought before the Sanhedrin. (This is the highest judicial council of Judaism, presided over by the high priest, with seventy-one members and located in Jerusalem.)[16]

"For I am a great King, says the LORD of hosts, and my name will be feared among the nations."

—Malachi 1:14

Read Mark 14:53–65, and then answer the questions that follow.

What did the high priest ask Jesus and how did Jesus answer, according to verses 61–62?

What happened next? Fill in the blanks based on the events in the text.

The high priest tore his ______________.

The high priest accused Jesus of ________________.

The council condemned Jesus to ___________.

What do you make of the high priest's actions? Do they seem sincere? Contrived? Share your thoughts.

We could easily spend an entire day of study examining the numerous rules that were broken at Jesus's "trial." The council's disregard for God's laws culminated with the high priest tearing his garments. Most often, this would be a sincere sign of deep mourning or sorrow. In this case, however, his actions conveyed an outward display of righteous indignation, but his true motive may have been to coax the other members to agree with his charge of blasphemy. One commentary author writes, "The *rending of the clothes* plainly shows how boldly and wickedly those who profanely despise God make false pretensions of zeal. . . . [T]his treacherous hypocrite . . . assumed a character which did not belong to him."[17]

"Hypocrite," as used by Jesus in the New Testament, is translated from the Hebrew verb *hanepu*, meaning "godless" (Jer. 23:11; also translated "defiled" or "polluted" as in Num. 35:33 and Isa. 24:5). Only later did the Greek word come to mean play-actor, or one who wears a mask.[18]

After being condemned to death, Jesus was taken to Pilate, the Roman governor who asked Jesus plainly, "Are you the King of the Jews?" In fact, the expression "King of the Jews" appears a full five times (with a sixth, "King of Israel") in Mark's account of Jesus being condemned to death and crucified (Mark 15:1–32). However, it is John's Gospel that traces this specific tragic thread to its final conclusion.

Read John 19:14-16. What do the chief priests declare, and what does this say about their allegiance to God, who is the *King of Israel* (Isa. 44:6)?

You may be familiar with the Gospel accounts of Christ's crucifixion: the horrifying beatings, the flogging, and the cruel soldiers who clothe Him in a purple robe and crown of thorns.[19] Mocking and spitting, they salute Him, "Hail, King of the Jews!" before they strip Him naked[20] and nail Him to the cross. Then, all four Gospel writers record the fact that the soldiers divided Jesus's garments and cast lots for His clothing—but John mentions something else.

Read John 19:23-24. How is the tunic described and what did the soldiers do with it?

Each of the four soldiers cast lots for one of five items of clothing. In addition to the tunic, which served as an undergarment, these most likely included sandals, an outer robe, a head cloth, and a belt. After casting lots, the tunic remained. Though drenched in blood, it was considered valuable because it was seamless; as such, it would have been foolish to tear it. The event fulfills the prophecy in Psalm 22:18. Yet the intact, simple undergarment, soiled with Christ's blood, sweat, and tears, also serves as a vivid contrast against the hypocritical tearing of the elaborate and pristine outer garment of the high priest.

Jesus's sinless life was a perfect reflection of His holy nature. He needed no defenders; He made no defense. Whereas the high priest clothed himself in costly, ornate robes and exploited the people for personal gain, Jesus gave everything—even His last shred of clothing, even His own blood—to save people from their sin. One scholar writes, "The one perfect life that has been lived in this world is the life of Him who owned nothing, and who left nothing but the clothes He wore."[21]

(Optional: you may enjoy reading the following poem, which I wrote one day as I rested with God at the ocean—my favorite place for a date with Jesus.)

In His Presence
Mighty waves—
gentle enough to soothe the weary soul.

Oh, to drink the depths of Your love—
to know the vastness of Your Presence.

You are always with me—
a river that overflows
with a peace no human heart can fully grasp.

I cling to You, my God and my Savior—
for Your mighty power sustains me
and Your gentle waters refresh me.

If I could count the ocean's tears,
would they do justice to the depths of Your love
for a dying world drowning in sorrows?

For the world knows You not.

Yet the ocean, in all its caverns filled,
cannot compare to a single drop of Your blood,
which purchased lost sinners and rescued them from the deep—
from deep waters where there was no one to help.

You ransomed my heart from a pool of sorrows—
for that was Your good pleasure.

You command the waters, "be still," and You calm my aching heart
as violence and fear flee from me.

You alone command the seas and set their boundaries.
You bind the enemy and make a decree, "you shall not cross,"
and he must obey.

For Your Word is Power—
You have power to give
and power to take away.

For all the world belongs to You—
the earth and everything in it is Yours.

Praise Your Name!

Your Turn

Think back upon the events we studied in Genesis in Week One when God made garments of animal skin to cover Adam and Eve's external shame. Now read Isaiah 61:10 in the margin. What does it mean to you to be "clothed in garments of salvation" and "covered in robes of righteousness"?

"I will greatly rejoice in the LORD; my soul shall exult in my God, for he has clothed me with the garments of salvation; he has covered me with the robe of righteousness." —Isaiah 61:10

What difference has it made in your life? How has God changed you from the inside out?

Who might God want you to share this wonderful truth with?

Lesson Summary

What Scripture, statement, or thought was most significant to you this week? Write it down and then reword it into a prayer of response to God.

Remember to visit www.shadiahrichi.com/bonus to access the worship playlist along with other great free resources.

Notes

[1] R. Jamieson, A. R. Fausset, and D. Brown, *Commentary Critical and Explanatory on the Whole Bible* (Oak Harbor, WA: Logos Research Systems, 1997), s.v. "Mark 5:27."

[2] The seven participles that occur between the identity of the woman and her action of touching Jesus comprise the following list.

"And there was a woman

- who had a discharge of blood for twelve years,
- and who had suffered much under many physicians,
- and had spent all that she had,
- and was no better
- but rather grew worse.
- She had heard the reports about Jesus
- and came up behind him in the crowd and touched his garment."

[3] A generic reference to "daughters of Jerusalem" is also spoken by Jesus as recorded in Luke 23:28.

[4] The Old Testament law did not specifically forbid an unclean person from touching a clean person; rather, the law warned that if a clean person touched the unclean, the clean person became unclean (Lev. 15:19–25). Nevertheless, it is certainly implied that intentionally risking defiling a person—especially a priest or other man of God—is a serious offense, as it would render the person unclean and thereby separate him or her from God for the prescribed period of time.

[5] See Deuteronomy 32:39; Job 2:6; Psalm 90:3, 139:16; and Revelation 1:18.

[6] Satan means "adversary." R. L. Thomas, "Satan," *New American Standard Hebrew-Aramaic and Greek Dictionaries,* updated ed. (Anaheim: Foundation Publications, 1998), 7854.

[7] In the original Greek, both "glory" and "dominion" are preceded by a definite article "the." In other words, the author is emphasizing *the* glory and *the* dominion—as in, there is no other.

[8] Study Notes, *The ESV Study Bible* (Wheaton, IL: Crossway Bibles, 2008), 2364.

[9] A deeper exploration into the temptations of Jesus can be found in my Bible study *Hagar: Rediscovering the God Who Sees Me.*

[10] R. Dean Jr. and T. Ice, *What the Bible Teaches about Spiritual Warfare* (Grand Rapids, MI: Kregel Publications, 2000), 60.

[11] Dean and Ice, *What the Bible Teaches about Spiritual Warfare*, 74.

[12] Whether the number one thousand is literal or figurative is debated among scholars. Either way, there will be an extensive period where Jesus reigns on the same earth currently in existence. Then the end will come, and He will "create a new heaven and a new earth" where righteousness reigns forever (Rev. 21).

[13] Very likely, this commander is the preincarnate Christ. First, when Joshua worships the visitor, the visitor does not object. Second, the commander speaks to Joshua in the same manner as the angel of the Lord spoke to Moses in Exodus 3:5 when He commanded Moses to remove his sandals because he was standing on holy ground. Finally, God is described in the Old Testament as the Lord of hosts, which is tantamount to calling Him commander of God's army.

[14] Of course, God does not need anything or anyone, but for His own pleasure and purposes, He created angels to serve as His agents and participate in His sovereign purposes.

[15] Yet, even here, we recognize that God's aim hasn't changed, which is that people would repent and turn to Him ("but they would not repent"; see Rev. 9:20–21 and 16:9–11).

[16] W. A. Elwell and B. J. Beitzel, "Sanhedrin," in *Baker Encyclopedia of the Bible*, vol. 2 (Grand Rapids, MI: Baker Book House, 1988), 1902.

[17] J. Calvin and W. Pringle, *Commentary on a Harmony of the Evangelists Matthew, Mark, and Luke*, vol. 3 (Bellingham, WA: Logos Bible Software, 2010), 258.

[18] H. L. Ellison, "Hypocrite," in *New Bible Dictionary*, 3rd ed., ed. D. R. W. Wood et al. (Downers Grove, IL: InterVarsity Press, 1996), 493.

[19] For a detailed exploration into Christ's Passion Week, you may enjoy Week Six, "Witnessing God's Passion," of my Bible study *Hagar: Rediscovering the God Who Sees Me*.

[20] Out of respect, artists who depict Jesus on the cross typically include a garment. However, the reality is that criminals were stripped naked and then crucified.

[21] J. R. Denney, *The Epistle to the Thessalonians* (London: Hodder and Stoughton, 1892), 78.

NOTES

NOTES

PART III

THE BLESSING

NOTES

WEEK SIX

ENTERING GOD'S REST

CAN YOU BELIEVE THIS IS OUR LAST WEEK? TAKE A MOMENT to appreciate how hard you have worked to reach this point. In the same way you may have encountered challenges as you journeyed through this study, the journey through life can also be challenging. However, just like this final week of our study, in life, the best is yet to come. God promises us in His Word, "There remains a Sabbath rest for the people of God" (Heb. 4:9). Today, we begin our final week, "Entering God's Rest."

"Even though I walk through the valley of the shadow of death, I will fear no evil, for you are with me." —Psalm 23:4

DAY ONE
Recognizing the King

"Today you will be with me in paradise."

—Jesus

Read Luke 23:32–43.

Try to imagine that you have lived most of your adult life as a criminal. There may be myriad reasons that led you down this path. Perhaps you suffered a painful childhood or grew up feeling like you never fit in. Maybe you wrestled with depression, or anger, or fear. Or it could be that you enjoyed the thrill of getting away with your crimes. Maybe long ago you simply rebelled, thinking that life (or God) had dealt you an unfair hand.

Regardless of what led to the poor choices you made, one day, your past finally catches up with you and you are led away to be crucified. You are not surprised that the only people standing at the foot of your cross are your executioners; your family and friends abandoned you years ago. Your partner in crime begins to mock the bloodied preacher-man stretched out between you. At first you join in, following his lead as you always have, but then the guilt sets in. In shame, you confess your sins and even begin to defend the man—the One they call the Christ. At last you turn, weighed down with guilt and shame; you can only hope, *remember me.*

"I will not forget you. Behold, I have engraved you on the palms of my hands."
—Isaiah 49:15–16

Right then, the preacher-man turns toward you with love in His eyes and blood dripping from his brow. And for the first time in perhaps a lifetime, you are welcomed with open arms. "Today you will be with me in paradise." To me, this is the most moving scene in the tragedy (and triumph) of the cross.

Consider the exchange between Jesus and the criminal. List everything the criminal acknowledged, based on his words in Luke 23:40–42.

Jesus responds, promising paradise. What did the criminal do that may have influenced Jesus's response? Circle all that apply.

He promised to change his ways.

He gave gifts to the poor.

He confessed his guilt.

He prayed a certain prayer.

He invested his life in serving God.

He acknowledged Jesus as King.

Although this exchange between the criminal and Jesus totals a mere four verses, like the story of Legion, it is perhaps one of the most beautiful displays of God's mercy in the four Gospels. The man knew he was guilty and deserved to die. He feared God and confessed his sin. He acknowledged the very words carved above Jesus's thorn-pierced brow: "This is the king of the Jews." But he never imagined that he could be forgiven.

What one thing did the criminal ask Jesus to do for him?

What might the man's request reveal about:

The man's heart?

The man's understanding of God, sin, or judgment?

Glance back at Mark 1:15. Fill in the missing words, based on Jesus's proclamation.

"The ___________ of God is at hand; _________ and believe in the gospel."

Jesus Is Enough

Sometimes we make things too complicated. The gospel, at its core, is simple: God has a kingdom, and those who enter are those who recognize His authority and sincerely repent of their sins. The criminal had no opportunity to live for God. No second chance to "turn his life around." The man knew he had spent his life in rebellion of God, and in his sorrow all he could bring himself to ask was for Jesus to "remember me."

Hanging on a cross and condemned to die, he had nothing to offer King Jesus. But the beauty of the gospel is this: Jesus did not come to seek an offering from us—He came to give an offering—*Himself*. And this is what makes this story so wonderful. The man acknowledged Jesus as King and repented of his sin—and that was enough.

"Today, you will be with me in paradise."

The beauty of the gospel is this: Jesus did not come to seek an offering from us–He came to give an offering–*Himself*.

Pause to Ponder

What does the word "paradise" mean to you? How would you describe paradise?

The word "paradise" occurs only three times in the New Testament (Luke 23:43; 2 Cor. 12:3; Rev. 2:7). The word was taken from an ancient Persian word describing a walled garden—particularly royal parks of kings.[1] Throughout the Old Testament and into the early New Testament period, the concept of an afterlife among God's people was fairly vague. The Jews "thought in terms not of heaven and of hell but of a shadowy world."[2] Only after Jesus was raised from the dead did the concept of the afterlife begin to come into focus.

In Week One, we explored how, in the beginning, God blessed humanity with:

- A beautiful paradise (Garden of Eden)
- Immortality (through the Tree of Life)
- The joy of God's presence

In the same way, when Jesus spoke to the criminal on the cross, He promised him (and all who accept His words) that he would enter:

- A beautiful paradise
- Life after death
- The presence of Jesus, the King

Truly, here is our first glimpse into the Lord's astounding promise that He will make all things new (Isa. 65:17; Rev. 21:1–4).

Imagine Jesus is speaking to you right now. Read Jesus's words below out loud five times, each time placing particular emphasis on one of the underlined words or phrases.

<u>Today</u>, <u>you</u> <u>will</u> be <u>with me</u> in <u>paradise</u>.

Which part of Jesus's promise stirs your heart the most? Why?

"Behold, the dwelling place of God is with man. He will dwell with them, and they will be his people, and God himself will be with them as their God."

—Revelation 21:3

True Paradise

As I read Jesus's promise and focus on the different aspects of it, each one speaks to my heart in a different way, as I imagine they do for you. Truly, these are beautiful words spoken by our Savior to a broken soul without any hope.

For me personally, in this season of my life, I think I am most moved by the fact that Jesus promises, "you will be *with me* in paradise." Jesus could simply have said, "Today, you will be in paradise." After all, isn't paradise what the world is longing for? But there is only one thing that makes true paradise so glorious: being in the arms of Jesus, being in the presence of God, our Savior and King.

Consider once again our story of the man with the legion. After Jesus healed the man, what *one thing* did the man request from Jesus when Jesus was about to leave? Circle one. (Hint: glance back at Mark 5:18.)

a mission   health and happiness   to be with Him   eternal life

How does Jesus's promise to the man on the cross offer hope to all who long to *be with* Jesus?

Both the story of the demoniac and that of the criminal on the cross serve as potent lessons in God's power to rescue and His heart of mercy. In the space below, share how each story serves in this way. I have completed one for you.

How does the person's story reflect God's power to rescue?	How does the person's story reflect God's heart of mercy?
Demoniac: Not even an army of demons can undermine God's plan to rescue!	Demoniac:
Criminal:	Criminal:

Pause to Ponder

How about you? How does your life's story reflect:

- God's power to rescue?
- God's heart of mercy?

You and I are rescued *from* God *by* God.

The truth is that all of us are in need of deliverance. As sinners, we all need rescue from God's holy wrath and righteous judgment. At the same time, as lost children, we all need the mercy found only in His loving arms. The astounding reality is that you and I are rescued *from* God *by* God. And this rescue was planned even before time began (Eph. 1:3–4; 2 Tim. 1:9–10). Jesus came to earth on a rescue mission—not because He had to, but because He planned to.

The Riches of His Grace

Slowly read the Scriptures listed below. What *one* thing stands out to you the most in each passage? Why do you think that is?

Ephesians 2:1–5

Ephesians 2:6–10

The apostle Paul certainly packs a lot into these ten verses. It does not matter whether you and I have lived our whole lives in perfect morality as measured by the world's standards—or even as measured by God's law.[3] Scripture teaches that apart from Jesus, all follow "the prince of the power of the air" and are "by nature children of wrath" and "sons of disobedience." For some, that's a hard truth to swallow, but God's Word does not lie. The prophet Jeremiah reminds us that "the heart is deceitful above all things" (17:9).

But there is good news! God, in His great love and mercy, rescued us from our sin through the blood of His Son Jesus—even our faith to turn to God is a gift.[4] This is why the story of the man with the legion (and others, like the thief on the cross) has so much to teach us. Jesus did not come down from Heaven to condemn, but to save (John 3:17).

No one knows how or why the demoniac became captive to a legion of demons; but *how* or *why* he came to his helpless state did not seem to concern Jesus. The same is true for the thief on the cross. Why or how these men came to be what they were did not matter to Jesus. It's not that Jesus loved them just the way they were; rather, He loved them *despite* the way they were. No condemnation, just mercy. And in the same way that the man with the legion was helpless to save himself, so was the criminal—*and so are we.*

Your Turn

As I shared earlier, the beauty of the gospel is this: Jesus did not come to seek an offering from us—He came to give an offering—*Himself.* None of us can earn God's favor. It makes no difference how many church services we attend, how much money we give to the poor, or how well our lives measure up to God's law (as if any of us could). When done from a sincere heart, those things are simply the natural outcome of a life already abandoned to God. We are His children solely due to His grace through faith in His Son Jesus, who paid our debt of sin on the cross.

Take a few moments to ask God if you might still be trying to earn His favor in some way. If so, how might this striving be holding you back in your walk with God, and what steps do you need to take to overcome it?

If you do not sense this is a struggle right now, write a prayer of gratitude for God giving you victory in this area.

DAY TWO

Jesus Has Won the Victory!

From the beginning of Mark's Gospel to the end, the demise of demonic forces is emphasized again and again. While the Jewish people in Jesus's day were certainly longing for their Messiah, they expected an immediate earthly kingdom. When Jesus arrived, however, He came casting out demons and announcing the good news that the kingdom of God was near.

"[H]e who is in you is greater than he who is in the world." —1 John 4:4

After Jesus triumphed over sin and death on the cross, He did not immediately establish a physical, earthly kingdom. Rather, He *inaugurated* the kingdom of God on earth—reestablishing His rule and reign over all creation, which humanity had tragically forfeited in that garden paradise so long ago. From there, Jesus's kingdom would grow slowly and exponentially, like a seed sown in a field. Then, at just the right time, He would return and complete the redemption and restoration of His creation.[5]

However, in the spiritual realm, where God exists outside of time, the fullness of Christ's triumph over all demonic forces is already accomplished.

Read Ephesians 1:19-23, which is printed below, and then answer the questions that follow.

> . . . according to the working of his great might that he worked in Christ when he raised him from the dead and seated him at his right hand in the heavenly places, far above all rule and authority and power and dominion, and above every name that is named, not only in this age but also in the one to come. And

> he put all things under his feet and gave him as head over all things to the church, which is his body, the fullness of him who fills all in all.

When Jesus was raised from the dead, where did He go?

What does it mean for us that Christ is raised and seated above all rule and authority?

Circle each occurrence of the words "all" and "every." How many times do these words appear in the text?

Is there any demon, ruler, or power that is not subject to Jesus's authority?

How can you take comfort in this truth?

The word "hell" (or *Gehenna* in Greek) comes from *ge innom* in Hebrew, which refers to the Valley of Hinnom—a valley near Jerusalem where children were sacrificed by fire in pagan worship.[8]

SUPPLEMENTAL READING

What Are Hades and the Abyss?

The Greek word *abyssos*, taken from the Hebrew word "deep," is often translated "bottomless pit" in the New Testament. In the Old Testament, "the deep" is a reference to the primeval sea (Gen. 1:2) or the ocean depths[6] (Ps. 33:7, 77:16), which were considered both dangerous and chaotic. The word was also used symbolically for the place of departed souls—that is, the grave, or *Sheol* in Hebrew. An example is Psalm 71:20, which reads, "You who have made me see many troubles and calamities will revive me again; from the depths of the earth you will bring me up again."

When we reach the New Testament, these concepts begin to gain further clarity and distinction. For example, in Revelation 17:8 and 20:1–3, the bottomless pit is not a reference to what we often understand as hell—the *final* place of judgment—but instead it seems to represent a temporary prison for evil spirits.[7]

Hades, on the other hand, is not the place of judgment. Rather, it refers to the realm of the dead (departed spirits) or, simply, the grave.[9] The dead can include believers, unbelievers, or both, depending on the context in which the word is used. *Gehenna* (hell), however, always refers to a place of judgment.[10]

The Darkest Day

". . . and darkness was over the face of the deep . . . " (Gen. 1:2).

There was darkness over the whole land . . . (Mark 15:33).

"The earth was without form and void . . ." (Gen. 1:2).

And the earth shook, and rocks were split . . . (Matt. 27:51).

In biblical times, natural phenomenon were understood as part of God's activity in the world. Earthquakes, for example, were associated with God's power and wrath (Exod. 19:18; Job 9:5–6; Ps. 18:7). Even darkness held meaning. Because God is the author of light and life, darkness was associated with the realm of the dead (Job 10:21–22, 38:17; Ps. 107:10, 14). Consequently, concerning the events surrounding Christ's crucifixion, "when darkness [and] earthquake . . . accompanied the death of Jesus, Jews of his day would have feared the end of the world—the victory of chaos."[11]

In fact, the darkest day on earth surely must have seemed a victory to our vile enemy Satan, but nothing could have been further from the truth. Perhaps he had forgotten God's pronouncement of his demise so long ago in that perfect garden paradise, but God did not (Gen. 3:15).

Read Colossians 2:15 in the margin and rewrite it using your own words.

"He disarmed the rulers and authorities and put them to open shame, by triumphing over them in him [through the cross]."

—Colossians 2:15

In Colossians 2:15, the "rulers and authorities" represent demonic powers (see 1 John 3:8 and Heb. 2:14). In biblical times, when a king returned from battle victorious, he would parade his enemy captives through the streets stripped naked, putting them to further shame (Isa. 20:4). The Greek word translated "disarmed" in Colossians 2:15 includes the idea of "stripped" or "taking off." Therefore, when Jesus triumphed over sin and death on the cross, not only were the demonic forces relieved of their weapons, but they were completely stripped of their power and position.

What difference does it make that the demonic forces have been "disarmed"?

What difference does it make to *you*?

It Is Finished

"And on the seventh day God finished his work . . ." (Gen. 2:2).

> *"It is finished," and he bowed his head and gave up his spirit . . .* (John 19:30).

There is perhaps no sweeter declaration ever uttered on this earth than what was exhaled in Jesus's final breath. *It is finished.*

Think back to our study in Genesis in Week One. On what day during creation week did God breathe life into Adam and bring both Adam and Eve into existence? (Hint: see Genesis 1:27, 2:7.)

Why was this significant? (Hint: glance back at page 24.)

Read Deuteronomy 5:12, 15. What reason is given in verse 15 as to why God's people were to observe the Sabbath?

Now read Mark 15:37, 42. On what day was Jesus crucified?

Finally, in John 19:30, we read Jesus's last words: "It is finished."[12] What might Jesus be referring to? List as many possibilities as you can think of.

Just as when God breathed life into humanity at the dawn of creation, and followed it with the blessing of entering into the first Sabbath rest in His presence, God paved the way for *eternal* rest—*eternal life!*—by opening heaven's door on the cusp of the most blessed Sabbath day. "Today, you will be with me in paradise."

Pause to Ponder

Read Mark 15:37 and Genesis 2:7. God is the giver of life, both physical and spiritual. Whereas God's breath is first poured *in* for man's physical life, His last breath is poured *out* for man's eternal soul. How does this speak to you personally?

And the Veil Was Torn

Read Mark 15:38. Whether or not you have read or heard teaching on this passage, what might the tearing of the temple curtain have meant to the Jews at that time?

Many scholars agree that the tearing of the massive veil guarding the entrance to the holy of holies represents the precious truth that the old sacrificial system is fulfilled in Christ. Man now has direct access to God through the perfect sacrifice of His Son. However, none of the Gospel writers includes this teaching. That understanding came later. In fact, there is no real reason to believe that the observers at the time would have recognized its symbolism in that way. So what might the torn veil have meant to them? Let's look at some parallels in Scripture to see if they can offer some insights.

Reread Mark 15:38 and continue through verse 39; then reread Mark 1:10–11. What similarities do you notice?

Now go back and reread Mark 14:61–63 and compare it with Mark 15:38. What symbolism might be at play here?

There are several interesting parallels in Mark's Gospel that are worth pondering. At the same time, we want to be careful not to make any conclusions that we cannot back up with Scripture. One author and professor of biblical studies offers this moving illustration:

> In the biblical world, the rending of garments signified mourning and sorrow. Perhaps, then, with the rip, Mark is showing God's response to his Son's death. If so, after Jesus cries out in anguish before his Father, the Father responds by tearing the curtain—his veritable garment—as an outcry of his own grief.[13]

Personally, I love this image. Given Mark's repeated mention of clothing throughout his Gospel (we only touched on a few), it may very well be that Mark expects his audience to make the connection. While we cannot be certain, we

"Oh that you would rend the heavens and come down, that the mountains might quake at your presence." —Isaiah 64:1

do know that God loves His Son (John 17:23) and draws near to those who suffer (Ps. 34:18).

Often the literary structure of a passage or even a whole book can provide additional insights. Picture the baptism of Jesus as portrayed at the beginning of Mark's Gospel. Mark describes "the heavens being torn open" and a voice from heaven declaring, "You are my beloved Son." This scene provides a striking parallel near the end of Mark's Gospel with the tearing of the temple veil and the centurion's astonished pronouncement: "Truly this man was the Son of God!"

When we consider the fact that, apart from demons, these are the only two in Mark's Gospel who acknowledge Jesus as the Son of God,[14] we begin to see the beauty that Mark weaves through his story. The first human in Mark's Gospel to proclaim Jesus as God's Son is a Roman executioner. The first evangelist is a restored Gentile demoniac. But there is another amazing first in this story.

Read Mark 16:9. (Optional: read 16:1–11.) How is Mary described? Why might Mark have chosen to point out this one particular fact about Mary? (Hint: How might it contribute to Mark's Gospel as a whole?)

While all four Gospels mention Mary Magdalene being at the empty tomb and seeing Jesus after He rose from the dead, only Mark includes a description of Mary as having once been possessed by demons. Both Mary and the man delivered from the legion were living proof of Jesus's power over demonic forces. From the very first chapter of Mark to the very last, we see the triumphant emphasis on Jesus's power over demons. And just as Jesus chose the man freed from the legion to be the first to proclaim Him as Lord, Jesus chose Mary to be the first to declare that He rose from the grave (Mark 16:10–11)—proving that Jesus is Lord both in this life *and* in the one to come.

Your Turn

It is finished! Sin, Satan, and death are defeated and Jesus has won the victory! The Bible assures us that because of Christ Jesus, "who died . . . who was raised—who is at the right hand of God . . . we are more than conquerors through him who loved us" (Rom. 8:34, 37; see also Eph. 1:20–21).

What can you do to hold on to these truths when you face difficulties or uncertainty?

Think back over the past year. How have you experienced Jesus's victory over sin or the forces of evil in your own life? Write a prayer of gratitude in the margin or in the notes pages.

Day Three

Trusting Him Who Holds the Keys

I have a painted sign on my front door that reads, "Be still, and know that I am God. —Psalm 46:10." It is a comforting verse, which is what attracted me to it as I was browsing in a Christian bookstore many years ago. Then one day, I read the full psalm. Earthquakes. Tidal waves. And that was just the beginning. Wars. Desolation. Fire. To say that the passage was not what I expected is quite an understatement.

However, in the midst of all the chaos depicted in this short psalm, God assures us that He is our refuge: "Be still, and know that I am God." The tiny phrase "be still" in Hebrew is not passive, but rather it's an active verb meaning to "stop" or "let go." Taken in context, God is imploring us to *let go* of our fears (verse 2) and *hold on* to Him because He is our fortress, refuge, and strength (verses 1, 7). Let's be honest: if you and I were facing wars and earthquakes and fire, it would be hard to "stop" and "let go"—*unless we were certain that God was in control.*

Who Is in Control?

Satan knows that he is powerless to steal a Christian's salvation, but he will stop at nothing to do the next best thing: to rattle our faith by undermining our understanding of who God is—the Sovereign Ruler of the universe to whom belongs all power, dominion, and authority. From the beginning of time until today, Satan has whispered all kinds of false teaching into the ears of God's children. His aim is to raise questions that cast doubt on God's sovereignty and unsettle our faith. Until we bring these into the light, you and I will remain vulnerable to Satan's lies.

Several of these questions center on what actually happened between Jesus's crucifixion and His resurrection. While an in-depth exploration into these topics is beyond the scope of this study, we will briefly tackle two of the more frequently raised questions in today's lesson. The first question deals with whether Jesus descended into hell after he died. The second relates to the idea that Jesus fought Satan in order to win back the keys of death and the grave (Rev. 1:18). Let's take a look.

Did Jesus Descend into Hell?

This question has confused and unsettled many. The notion stems from just a few verses in Scripture, primarily 1 Peter 3:19, Revelation 1:18, and, to a lesser extent, Ephesians 4:9, which reads, "In saying, 'He ascended,' what does it mean but that he had also descended into the lower regions, the earth?" This verse is likely the basis for the phrase that Christ "descended into hell" as written in the Apostle's Creed centuries ago.[15] Today, however, many biblical scholars interpret Ephesians 4:9 as simply referring to Christ's incarnation and/or His death, including His descent into Hades (or the grave),[16] rather than into hell (the final place of judgment).[17]

Let's look at 1 Peter 3:19. (We will explore Revelation 1:18 in the next section.)

Read 1 Peter 3:18–22 to get an overview of the passage. What do you suppose the following three objects might represent? List all the possibilities you can think of.

The spirits:

The prison:

The message proclaimed:

This passage is challenging to interpret, due in no small part to the variety of opinions as to what the spirits may be (possibilities include all unbelieving departed souls, only those souls who perished in the flood, or even demons). Nevertheless, there are several clues that can help shed some light. First, the English word translated "proclaim" (or "preach") appears four times in Peter's letter. In three of those instances (1 Pet. 1:12, 1:25, 4:6), Peter uses the Greek verb *euangelizo*. In all three usages (as well its occurrence throughout the New Testament), the word relates to *preaching the good news* of God's kingdom.[18] However, in 1 Peter 3:19, Peter uses the verb *kerusso*, which simply means to tell or announce something. While other New Testament authors also commonly use this verb in regard to preaching the good news, because the context surrounding 1 Peter 3:19 is not the announcement of good news, but rather of judgment, Peter chooses the broader verb *kerusso*.

Another key word in the passage is the word "prison."

Pause to Ponder

> When you think of the word "prison," what comes to mind? How would you describe it?

The word "prison" in Greek stems from the verb "to guard" and refers to a holding cell for criminals. Prison is not synonymous with hell, however, as hell always refers to a place of *final* judgment and *eternal* punishment (Matt. 5:22, 10:28; Mark 9:43; Luke 12:5). In the book of Revelation, hell is also symbolically referred to as the "lake of fire" (19:20 and 21:8). If 1 Peter 3:19 does mean that Jesus Himself "proclaimed to the spirits in prison" after His death, the location of the prison would not be in hell, but in *hades*. (See yesterday's Supplemental Reading, "What Are Hades and the Abyss?" on page 194.)

However, there is something in the passage that brings into question the idea that this preaching took place after Jesus's death. The verse reads that Jesus was "made alive in the spirit, *in which* he went and proclaimed to the spirits in prison. . . ." The words "in which" may suggest a different interpretation, even a different time period, since the Spirit of God is not bound by time or space. Because there is no consensus on who the "spirits" are, some scholars have sought to untangle the passage by examining the "proclaiming" itself—namely, what was proclaimed and when. Those who hold that this proclaiming occurred between Jesus's death and resurrection differ in opinion as to whether the message was directed to a group of imprisoned demons, all departed unbelieving souls, or merely those who lived in "the days of Noah" but rejected Noah's warning. However, other biblical scholars propose that the proclaiming may refer to the preaching of Noah himself, which occurred centuries before.

The authors of the ESV Bible Study Notes offer several compelling reasons for this interpretation. First, Peter describes Noah as a "herald of righteousness" (2 Pet. 2:5). The Greek word translated "herald" is *keryka*, which stems from the same verb Peter uses in 1 Peter 3:19, *kerusso*. Also, in chapter 1 (verses 10–11), Peter introduces his letter by saying that the "Spirit of Christ" was *speaking through the Old Testament prophets*, which ties in nicely with our passage in chapter 3. Finally, we always want to consider the context, which is a fundamental principle for proper biblical interpretation that cannot be overemphasized. The ESV Study Bible notes that the "context indicates that Christ was preaching through Noah, who was in a persecuted minority . . . which is similar to the situation in Peter's time. . . ."[19] In other words, because the current situation mirrors the days of Noah, it would

be natural for Peter to point his readers back to the preaching of Noah, and that may simply be all that is going on here.

In addition to all of this, we can glean even further observations from other Scriptures.

Read the verses listed below (some are a review). How do these shed light on the question of whether Jesus descended into hell?

1 Peter 3:22

John 19:28, 30

Luke 23:43

Luke 23:46

These passages are just a handful that support the idea that Jesus did not descend into hell after His death. Even more significant is the fact that there is not one Bible verse that plainly states Jesus *did* enter hell. Whenever we come across passages in Scripture that are difficult to interpret and about which respected biblical scholars disagree, it is always wise *not* to use these passages to formulate our theology. The best interpreter of Scripture is Scripture. Perhaps the most credible argument, then, against the idea that Jesus went to hell after His death are His own words declaring where He was headed next: "Today, you will be *with me* in paradise," and, in speaking to God the Father, "into your hands I commit my spirit." While we cannot be entirely certain as to everything that happened between Jesus's death and resurrection, we do know that even the grave could not hold Him!

Did Jesus Fight Satan to Win Back the Keys?

This is another question that can cast doubt on God's power and, to Satan's delight, fuel insecurity among believers. After all, if Jesus had to battle Satan and wrestle "the keys of Death and Hades" from Satan's hands, then either Satan is far mightier than we could imagine or Jesus is far weaker than we could ever fear. Before we tackle the specific passage in question, let's see what general principles we can extract from other Scriptures.

In our journey through Mark's Gospel, we explored many stories where Jesus encountered demons.

How did the demons respond to Jesus? Write T (true) or F (false) next to each description if the demons (either some or all) responded in this way.

______ Cowered in His presence

______ Obeyed His commands

______ Caused Jesus to become fearful

______ Recognized Him as God's Son

______ Were disobedient

______ Feared impending judgment

______ Fought with Jesus

______ Fell at His feet

"[T]he ruler of this world . . . has no claim on me"; "I have authority to lay [my life] down, and I have authority to take it up again." —John 14:30, 10:18

Next, read the verses from John's Gospel in the margin. What implication do these verses have for the idea that, prior to Jesus's resurrection, Satan held the authority ("the keys") over death and the grave?

Jesus declared in His dying breath, "It is finished." How does Jesus's own proclamation line up with the notion that Jesus needed to do battle with Satan afterward?

Finally, read Jude 9 and Revelation 12:7–9 and answer the questions that follow.

Who is Satan's opponent, according to these passages?

Does this surprise you? Why or why not?

What is the significance of this truth in light of the two questions that are the topic of today's lesson (see bottom of page 199)?

Even before we explore the verse regarding the "keys" in the book of Revelation, Scripture already provides us with tremendous insight. If, during Jesus's earthly life, Satan held some kind of power over Jesus, why did the demons cower in Jesus's presence, fear His judgment, and obey His commands? And if Jesus did not already possess authority over death and the grave, how could He declare authority to lay down his life and raise it up again? Perhaps one of the biggest misconceptions

fueling the confusion is that Satan is Jesus's rival, when, in fact, the only time[20] Scripture portrays Satan as being in an actual battle is when he fights against the angel Michael in heaven (Rev. 12:7–9). The fact is that Jesus has no rivals. He is the Son of God and Creator of the universe. Therefore, all of His creatures—humanity, angels, and fallen angels alike—are under His absolute authority.

Nevertheless, ever since humans handed their delegated authority over the earth to Satan, God, in His sovereignty, has allowed Satan a certain measure of freedom, within a fixed period of time, in order to accomplish *His* purposes. God rules over Satan by restraining Satan's activity (Job 1:12, 2:6; 2 Thess. 2:6–9), and in *His* perfect time will put an end to it altogether. The price Jesus paid on the cross to redeem humanity from sin and eternal damnation was not Satan's wrath, but *God's*. "Yet it was the will of the LORD to crush him . . . when his soul makes an offering for guilt" (Isa. 53:10).

We are saved by the *blood* of Jesus; not a battle, not a triumph over hell, but the *blood*.

Scripture teaches again and again that we are saved by the *blood* of Jesus; not a battle, not a triumph over hell, but the *blood*. The real "battle" for our souls was fought in the Garden of Gethsemane and accomplished on the cross. First, in the Garden, where Jesus initially begged His Father that the "cup" (the wrath of God) would be taken from Him. Finally, on the cross, where Jesus, having resolved in the garden to fulfill His mission, drank it.

The moment the sin-cursed earth drank the blood of the holy Son of God, all the powers of darkness—sin, Satan, and death—were forever defeated in a crushing victory. "It is finished."

Who Holds the Keys of Death and Hades?

"But God raised Him up again, putting an end to the agony of death, since it was impossible for Him to be held in its power."
—Acts 2:24 NASB

Read Acts 2:24 in the margin and John 10:18 in your Bible. What do these verses convey concerning Jesus's authority over death and the grave?

Now read Revelation 1:17-18. Complete the passage below, based on what Jesus declares about Himself (the identity of the speaker as Jesus is based upon verses 12-16).

I am the __________ and the last, and the living one.

I died, and behold I am alive __________,

and I have the __________ of Death and Hades.

Finally, read the following verses and fill in the missing word or phrases:

Isaiah 44:6 "I am the __________ and I am the last."

Isaiah 40:28 "The LORD is the __________ God."

In Revelation 1:17–18, Jesus makes several profound statements about Himself. All but one parallel other Scriptures describing God's *eternal* attributes.

Based on all of these truths, what conclusions can you draw about Jesus's possessing the "keys" of Death and Hades?

The reality is that Jesus is the living, eternal Son of God. If there were even one aspect of His divine power that He did not possess *at any given time*, then that "power" would have supremacy over God the Son, who, as the second person of the Trinity, is God Himself. In other words, that other "power" would be God. However, the very fact that Jesus passed into death, the grave (hades), and back out again, *proves* that even death and the grave have no power over Him.

In Revelation 1:18, Jesus did not say I *now* have the keys. Jesus is the eternal, living, Almighty God. He *always* had the keys. The concept that Satan had the keys at any point in time is simply incorrect. Satan's "power" over death and the grave, as we studied last week, relates to his enslavement of people to sin, and his accusations that they deserve death. Nothing more. God is, has been, and always will be the Sovereign Ruler over the universe, *including life and death.*

Your Turn

What aspect of today's lesson encourages you the most? Why?

With whom will you share what you have learned?

(Optional: We briefly studied the fact that we are saved not by a battle or the recovery of lost keys, but by the *blood* of Jesus. Consider setting aside some time to conduct a search for the word "blood" in the New Testament using a Bible concordance. Record all the blessings made available to you through the gift of Christ's blood.)

Before any human being took his first breath, God vowed a rescue mission.

"The highest form of selfishness is that of the man who is content to go to heaven alone."[24]

—J. C. Ryle

Day Four
Celebrating God's Patience

Long before any human being took his first breath, God vowed a rescue mission. God is faithful; He always finishes what He has started. Just as I can trust Him to carry me through these last days of writing, and you can trust Him to carry you through these last days of study, He is faithful to carry humanity through the last days of history and into our eternal rest: the beautiful paradise He planned for us so long ago. But until then, there is work to be done, and God calls each of us to partner with Him in seeing it to completion.

Read Mark 16:15–18. Consider the text carefully; what did Jesus *command* His disciples to do? Circle all that apply.

handle snakes   cast out demons   preach the gospel

speak different languages

Before Jesus ascended into heaven, He entrusted His eleven disciples with one mission: *preach the gospel.*[21] Concerning the subsequent verses of Mark 16:15–18, there is simply no consensus. Some scholars suggest that the imagery is symbolic for victory over the spiritual forces of evil in general (see Ps. 91:13; Luke 10:18–20). Others acknowledge the activity occurring at the beginning of church history,[22] but they hold that as the church grew, the need for such signs *in order to validate the message of the gospel* were no longer the norm.[23] This was due mainly to the fact that, by this point, the written Word of God was completed and the resurrection of Jesus confirmed by hundreds of eyewitnesses (1 Cor. 15:6). Before ascending into heaven, Jesus Himself said, "Blessed are those who have not seen and yet have believed" (John 20:29; see also 2 Cor. 5:7).

While various interpretations of the passage in Mark 16 have been proposed, Jesus's command remains the same: *preach the gospel.* From the beginning of human history until now, God has been on a rescue mission . . . and time is running out (Rev. 22:10).

Pause to Ponder

When did you first hear the good news? Who shared it with you? Did you respond immediately or did it take time? How was God patient with you (or how is God currently being patient with you) in your journey toward faith in Jesus Christ?

Noticing the One

It has never been about the masses with You, oh Lord; it has always been about the one. These are words I wrote in my journal several years ago. Throughout Jesus's earthly ministry, regardless of the crowds or activity swirling around Him, Jesus always noticed the one, such as:

- The paralytic lowered through the roof because of the crowds.
- The "unclean" woman daring to touch Jesus's garment.
- The condemned criminal at Jesus's side, asking, "Remember me."

And how can we forget the man with the legion? The one everyone else had given up on—everyone but Jesus, for He sees *behind the seen*. Determined to rescue him, Jesus sailed across a raging sea and confronted an army of demons. Truly, the story of Legion epitomizes the depths of God's love and how far He will go to rescue *one . . . lost . . . soul*. Again and again, Jesus demonstrated His desire to rescue the hurting, the broken, and the abandoned. In the same way, every soul you and I encounter in this life has infinite value to God.

Jesus always notices the one. In the same way, every soul you and I encounter in this life has infinite value to God.

Read Romans 10:13–15. Fill in the blanks with the missing words, based on the passage, from the last statement to the first.

How beautiful are the feet of those who preach the ________________!

[But] how are they to preach unless they are ________________?

And how are they to ________ without someone ________________?

And how are they to believe in him of whom they have never __________?

How then will they call on [the Lord] in whom they have not __________?

Next, circle every action verb in these five statements. What observations can you make?

Finally, recall the simplicity of the gospel message that Jesus preached by completing the sentence below. (Hint: reread Mark 1:15).

The time is fulfilled, and the __________ of God is at hand; __________ and believe in the gospel.

Pause to Ponder

Read Mark 13:9–11. While the context relates to being on trial before those in authority, this passage gives us comfort that the Holy Spirit will enable us to have the courage to speak the truth of the gospel in the midst of persecution. How have you experienced the Holy Spirit's enabling to be a witness for Christ when you knew doing so would be costly? What were the risks? What was the outcome? How did the experience impact your faith?

The Patience of God

She did not just pick up her cell phone, I thought to myself, incredulous. I had been waiting in line at the bank for more than twenty minutes. It was my turn next, and I had just remarked to the woman behind me that it seemed I was getting a lesson on patience—I was only half joking. Though there were a number of employees milling about, only one bank teller window was open. Finally, a second teller sat down at her window and removed the "next teller" sign, signaling that her window was open. No sooner did I take one step forward than she put the sign back and walked away to answer her cell phone. Judging by the smile on her face, the call was *not* an emergency.

Seriously? I began grumbling to myself. *Here I am with a boatload of work to do at my office, but instead I am stuck in this line.* It was at that moment I sensed God nudging my spirit. *Uh oh; this can't be good*, I nearly said out loud. When it seemed God was satisfied that He had my attention, He brought to my mind what He had revealed to me in His Word earlier that day. Then I remembered: *patience*. It wasn't something I read in the Psalms or Proverbs. It didn't come up in my study of Mark. I saw it in the story of the Exodus.

"[T]he people of Israel groaned because of their slavery and cried out for help. Their cry for rescue from slavery came up to God." —Exodus 2:23

Pause to Ponder

Looking back, in what ways has God extended patience toward you since you surrendered lordship of your life to King Jesus? If you have not yet surrendered your life to Jesus, what might be holding you back?

Sometimes God chooses to unfold His plan in stages; this is what we discover in the story of the Exodus. When God sent Moses to demand that Pharaoh let

His people go and Pharaoh refused, rather than wiping Egypt off the face of the earth (which He most certainly could have done), God implemented His rescue plan in stages—a series of plagues, each worse than the last. It began with water turning to blood, then an invasion of frogs, followed by swarms of insects. At one point, even Pharaoh's advisors began to plead with him to let the Israelites go (Exod. 10:7). Instead, the king of Egypt continued to defy the God of heaven.

The plagues intensified: painful sores and violent hailstones, until finally, locusts, darkness, and death. These plagues likely occurred over several months. During this time, the plagues hardened the heart of Pharaoh, but others responded differently.

Read Exodus 9:20. Describe those who heeded the warning to protect their slaves and livestock from the impending hailstorm. Be specific.

"The fear of the LORD is the beginning of knowledge; fools despise wisdom and instruction." —Proverbs 1:7

How does Exodus 9:20 illustrate God's mercy and patience in the midst of His judgments?

What general principles can you apply to your life?

PAUSE TO PONDER

In your opinion, how accurately does the description "[they] feared the word of the LORD" reflect Christians in our churches today? Place an X on the line to indicate your response.

not accurate — extremely accurate

Explain your response.

How about you? How accurately would you say the description reflects you?

not accurate — extremely accurate

Explain.

Read Exodus 12:38, 48–51, and then answer the questions that follow.

Who might the people be that joined the Israelites? List as many possibilities as you can think of.

How was Moses instructed to deal with those who joined God's community?

What do these events reveal about God's character?

"The Lord . . . is patient toward you, not wishing that any should perish, but that all should reach repentance." —2 Peter 3:9

No one disagrees that the Exodus is a miraculous story of God's power. However, few might consider that it is also a beautiful display of God's *patience*. By the time the Israelites left Egypt, many other people had attached themselves to God's nation. God parted the Red Sea not only for the Israelites but also for *all* who chose to follow. In the end, after Pharaoh became enraged, gathered his troops for battle, and pursued God's people into the wilderness, God simply cast the enemy into the sea, never to be seen or heard from again.

The Final Showdown

In Scripture, when God performs the miraculous, the event is rarely repeated, such as God speaking to Moses in the burning bush (Exod. 3:1–6) or the sun standing still until Israel's army defeated their enemies (Josh. 10:12–14). *Not so with the plagues.* Just as the drowning of Pharaoh's army foreshadows the drowning of the legion in a herd of pigs, the series of plagues in Egypt foreshadows a final showdown yet to come. The story appears in the book of Revelation.

Revelation was given to us by God to provide a glimpse into the "things that must soon take place" (Rev. 1:1)—human history's final chapters. While it is a challenging book to interpret, there are a handful of segments that we will explore today and tomorrow to help put what we have learned into perspective.

Optional: read Revelation 16:1–21.

In Revelation 16, which is very reminiscent of the plagues of Egypt, God executes a series of judgments with the same intention He has had from the beginning: to display His glory, and in doing so, draw people to Himself and lead them to repentance (Rev. 2:21; see also Gen. 3:8–9, Exod. 10:3, and Mark 1:15). Tragically, despite countless opportunities to embrace God's love and acknowledge

His sovereignty, like the Pharaoh in Exodus, the people "would not repent" (Rev. 16:9, 11). In fact, they cursed God (Rev. 16:9, 11, 21). While God's love and His incredible patience and mercy are infinite, there will come a day when the final chapter of human history will come to a close, and the opportunity to embrace His salvation will come to an end.

Read Revelation 19:11–13 and 19:19–20:3. (Optional: read 19:11–20:3.) Describe the "battle" in your own words. What happened? Be specific.

There is no consensus on the meaning of "Armageddon" (*Har Magedon*), and whether the conflict to occur there is literal or symbolic. If literal, most scholars hold that the name means Mount Megiddo, since the area was the scene of many key battles in Israel's history.[25]

Not. One. Shot. I can still remember my seminary professor stressing these words years ago as I sat in his class on Revelation. And it is true: Scripture never records that the enemy fired a single shot.[26] The expression "battle of Armageddon" is actually misleading. In truth, there was no battle. Though enemies *gathered* against King Jesus and His army for battle, the leaders were immediately captured, and the rest were "slain by the sword that came from the mouth of him who was sitting on the horse" (Rev. 19:21). Quite a humiliating defeat, I'd say. Even if the passage is taken figuratively, symbolizing a final worldwide conflict between good and evil,[27] the point of the passage is the same: King Jesus is victorious.

However, God is not finished. This is not the last chapter—of Revelation or the story of Legion.

Your Turn

How has God been patient with you this past week? How about this past year?

With God, everything has a purpose. What might He be aiming at in His patience toward you? What has it accomplished?

Write a prayer of praise recounting and celebrating God's kindness as demonstrated in His patience toward you.

Day Five
Resting on His Promises

"Seek the LORD while he may be found; call upon him while he is near."
—Isaiah 55:6

God is on a rescue mission. Ever since that first garden paradise when He called out, "Where are you?" God's heart has longed for all to turn to Him in humble repentance (2 Pet. 3:9). From the days of Noah to Moses, to Jesus, to today, God longs to welcome into His paradise all who will come to Him.

Paradise Lost

The news shocked everyone: Paradise, California, was on fire. I know several people who lost their homes and everything they owned except the clothes on their backs as they raced to escape the raging inferno. One of these friends contacted me and shared that she and her husband had been living in a motel for the past month. I cannot imagine the devastation of suddenly being homeless and losing everything. Surely the sense of "this is not how it was supposed to be" would be overwhelming. Yet, even in the midst of such loss, my friend shared with me how grateful to God they are to be alive.

Scripture reminds us that one day, each of us will leave this world behind. The book of Hebrews tells us that this world was never our permanent home. In fact, when God brought His people into the land of promise, even then it was not their final destination: "For if Joshua had given them rest, God would not have spoken of another day later on. So then, there remains a Sabbath rest for the people of God" (Heb. 4:8–9).

However, it seems that God prefers to usher in this rest in stages . . .

God Will Swallow Up Death Forever

Long ago, in that first garden paradise, God promised a Savior who would one day crush our enemy under His feet (Gen. 3:15), but that's not where the story ends. God also promises that He will create a new heaven and new earth (Isa. 65:17, 66:22). However, after Jesus defeats and imprisons[28] Satan (Rev. 20), rather than establishing His new earth right away, Scripture teaches that Jesus will first reign on the existing earth for one thousand years.[29] I don't know about you, but when I first read this years ago, I immediately wondered, *Why? What's the point?*

Read Revelation 20:7-10 (Optional: read verses 4-10). Compare this "battle" with the one in Revelation 19:19-21. What similarities do you notice?

Scripture reveals that, as Christians, we wrestle against three forces: the world, the flesh, and the devil (1 John 2:15–16; Gal. 5:16–17; 1 Pet. 5:8). However, for one thousand years, both the "world" (that is, the world system under the evil one) and the "devil" (Satan and his forces) are out of the way. All this time, Jesus is ruling the earth in righteousness and justice. Truly, this is a world as close to paradise as one can imagine this side of heaven. Nevertheless, people still rebel.

Consider the events briefly described in the previous paragraph. What do these events reveal about the human condition. What conclusions can you draw?

"For everyone who has been born of God overcomes the world. And this is the victory that has overcome the world—our faith." —1 John 5:4

Pause to Ponder

Read 1 John 5:4 in the margin. How can you take comfort in this truth? How have you experienced this truth in your own life?

It's a tragic commentary on the human condition: the minute Satan is freed from his prison, people join forces to rally with him against God, proving once and for all that even "world peace" and the absence of evil forces is not enough—*even one thousand years' worth!* The reality is that, apart from a supernatural transformation, the human heart is still plagued with sin (Rom. 6:6) and is "desperately wicked" (Jer. 17:9). With sin ruling in their hearts, the rebellious once again gather for battle, and once again, the enemy is defeated. This time, however, the punishment is final. Satan is thrown into the lake of fire—and just like the army of Pharaoh, he is never to be seen or heard from again.

But there is one last enemy to be dealt with.

Read 1 Corinthians 15:26 and Revelation 20:14. What do these verses promise?

"And he will swallow up on this mountain the covering that is cast over all peoples. . . . He will swallow up death forever; and the Lord God will wipe away tears from all faces." —Isaiah 25:7-8

Since death is not an independent being, how can it be an enemy? What might this mean? (Hint: What additional insight does Isaiah 25:7-8 in the margin provide?)

Pause to Ponder

How has death been an enemy to you? What does the promise in Revelation 20:14 mean to you personally?

The Promise of a New Heaven and a New Earth

Read Revelation 21:1-4 and 23-25. List every assurance promised in these verses.

Which of the truths listed are you most grateful for? Why?

There are so many things I look forward to when we will live in our eternal home. To experience the true "rest" that God planned for us (Heb. 4:8) means you and I will never suffer from nightmares or fears again. We will never again hide in shame or try to run from our past. All of our wounds, tears, and scars will be wiped away. In fact, the only scars in heaven will be on the body of our Lord to serve as a witness of His love for all eternity. These are the true "battle scars" of a Champion who came to earth to rescue Adam's race and usher God's beloved children into an eternal paradise.

Consider once again the promises in Revelation 21:1-4 and 23-35. Is there anything that surprises, puzzles, or even disappoints you? Explain.

I love living close to the ocean. In fact, I try to visit the beach once each week; I call it my "date with Jesus." And so I'll be honest: the first time I read in Revelation 21 that the sea will be "no more," I was disappointed. I didn't understand why God would omit something so wonderful from His new creation. However, much in the book of Revelation is symbolic, and so we cannot be certain exactly what this might mean. In describing what he sees, the apostle John often uses expressions such as it "looks like" or "appears to be"—in other words, the vision is so "other worldly" that no known words can convey it, and all John can do is try to compare it to something his readers would be familiar with.

Nevertheless, whatever the new earth will be like, of one thing we can be certain: no one will be disappointed. If our current earth, which is filled with violence and heartache and will one day be destroyed by fire (2 Pet. 3:10–12), still offers glimpses of profound beauty and wonderful experiences to enjoy in this life, how much more glorious will our *eternal* home be?

Actually, the statement "the sea was no more" (whether literal or figurative) might have been intended to bring comfort. In biblical times, the sea was considered dangerous and chaotic.[30] One commentary author explains that, in Revelation, the sea is used "as a symbol of chaos and may [even] symbolize evil. The beast came from the sea (Rev. 13:1). [And the] great harlot sits on many waters (Rev. 17:1)."[31] As we studied in Week One, before God created the world, "The earth was without form and void, and darkness was over the face of the deep" (Gen. 1:2a). However, our eternal home will be one of harmony, order, life, and light (Rev. 21:23–24, 22:2).

In fact, the description in Revelation 4:6 of the "sea of glass" before God's throne may suggest a body of water so calm that it resembles glass, even in the midst of the awesome power of God (Rev. 4:5). This imagery would serve as a stark contrast to the fearful violence and danger the sea represented at the time Revelation was written. Surely for Jesus's disciples, the memory of crossing the Sea of Galilee would immediately come to mind when, in the midst of a raging storm, Jesus rebuked the wind and the sea, and instantaneously "there was a great calm" (Mark 4:39).

Entrusted with a Mission

But we are not in paradise yet. As long as you and I have breath, like the man healed of the legion, we have been given an opportunity to display God's power and mercy through our stories and our lives. We can tell a world drowning in sorrow that there is a God who rescues—that there is a God who transforms our chaos into calm and our darkness into light.

Think back on the story of Legion, and then answer the following questions.
How did the townspeople initially respond to Jesus's presence? Circle one.
(Hint: glance back at Mark 5:17.)

Welcomed Him

Listened to His teaching

Begged Him to leave

Brought others to be healed

"But you are a chosen race, a royal priesthood, a holy nation, a people for his own possession, that you may proclaim the excellencies of him who called you out of darkness into his marvelous light. Once you were not a people, but now you are God's people; once you had not received mercy, but now you have received mercy."

—1 Pet. 2:9–10

How did the healed man respond to Jesus's command to go and "tell your friends"? Circle one. (Hint: glance back at Mark 5:20.) The man:

Promised to pray about it

Climbed into Jesus's boat

Proclaimed Jesus throughout the region

Bought a house and settled there

Read Mark 7:31 and 8:1–9. Summarize the events in your own words.

Next, compare and contrast these verses with Mark 5:20. What conclusions can you draw?

After Jesus healed the demoniac, He returned to the Decapolis roughly six months later.[32] Rather than rejection, a large crowd came and gathered—four thousand, in fact. They stayed with Jesus for so long (three days!) that Jesus performed a miracle to feed them all. Could the welcoming reception Jesus received be partly due to the faithfulness and obedience of *one* man—of the man rescued from the legion?

"... for whoever has entered God's rest has also rested from his works as God did from his."
—Hebrews 4:10

Coming Home

Let's pause here for a moment. Sit back, relax, and take a deep breath. Now, let your mind picture the scene. Imagine that *you* were among those who heard about Jesus through the testimony of the man healed from the legion. Though you never learned his name, you are forever grateful for his message. Years later, you enter paradise. When it is announced that the man who told you about Jesus is finally coming home, you, along with countless others, gather to stand behind Jesus. Each of you is eager to thank the man whose name you never knew—until now. You watch as the man enters. Immediately, he runs into Jesus's arms as Jesus declares, "Welcome home, my son! Well done, good and faithful servant." Then, with a smile that reaches into the depths of the man's soul, Jesus takes him by the hand as He leads him toward the crowd. "Come with me; there are some people I want you to meet. . . ."

Your Turn

Long before Jesus ever set foot on the other side of the Sea of Galilee, He saw what that man could never have dreamed: He saw the countless souls that his life would impact. Jesus saw *behind the seen*. And so Jesus commanded him, "Go home to your friends and tell them how much the Lord has done for you, and how he has had mercy on you." And just as He commissioned the healed man, Jesus commissioned His disciples, and He commissions us: "Go into all the world and proclaim the gospel to the whole creation"—tell them about the *God Who Rescues Me*.

"How beautiful are the feet of those who preach the good news!" (Rom. 10:15).

"And the seed that fell on good soil represents those who hear and accept God's word and produce a harvest of thirty, sixty, or even a hundred times as much as had been planted!"

—Mark 4:20 NLT

Lesson Summary

What Scripture, statement, or thought was most significant to you this week? Write it down and then reword it into a prayer of response to God.

Be sure to visit shadiahrichi.com/bonus to join my email community and gain access to all the great free resources! I look forward to connecting with you!

Notes

[1] W. A. Elwell and B. J. Beitzel, "Paradise," in *Baker Encyclopedia of the Bible*, vol. 2 (Grand Rapids, MI: Baker Book House, 1988), 1614.

[2] William Barclay, *The Letters of James and Peter*, 3rd ed. (Louisville, KY: Westminster John Knox Press, 2003), 273.

[3] Jesus shocked His disciples by teaching that "unless your righteousness exceeds that of the scribes and Pharisees, you will never enter the kingdom of heaven" (Matt. 5:20). God does not view a person based on his or her external behavior; God looks at the heart. Only a person whose heart is transformed by the blood of Christ can live a life that is truly pleasing to God.

[4] Some may wonder if it is grace, not faith (or salvation through faith), that is a gift. However, in Ephesians 2:9, the gift is described as "not a result of works." Since grace, by its very definition, can never be described in this way, it would appear to be faith (or salvation through faith) that Paul is referring to. (See also Philippians 1:29, 1 Peter 1:5.)

[5] Israel Steinmetz, "Kingdom-Focused Leadership," *Bible Advocate Magazine* 152, no. 6 (November–December 2018): 19.

[6] W. A. Elwell and B. J. Beitzel, "Bottomless Pit," in *Baker Encyclopedia of the Bible*, vol. 1 (Grand Rapids, MI: Baker Book House, 1988), 375.

[7] See also 2 Peter 2:4 where the word translated "hell" is actually *Tartarus*, taken from Greek mythology, and the verse continues, "to be kept until the judgment."

[8] D. K. Innes, "Hell," in *New Bible Dictionary*, 3rd ed., ed. D. R. W. Wood et al. (Downers Grove, IL: InterVarsity Press, 1996), 463.

[9] *The Lexham Bible Dictionary*, ed. J. D. Barry et al. (Bellingham, WA: Lexham Press, 2016), s.v. "Hades."

[10] *The Lexham Bible Dictionary*, s.v. "Hades."

[11] Michael S. Heiser, "Strange and Powerful Signs," *Bible Study Magazine* 9, no. 3 (March–April 2017): 40.

[12] Luke 23:46 adds the words, "Father, into your hands I commit my spirit!"

[13] Joseph R. Dodson, "A Decisive Rip," *Bible Study Magazine* 10, no. 3 (March–April 2018): 6.

[14] Mark does identify Jesus as Son of God at the introduction of his Gospel (1:1); however, I am referring here to the events Mark describes. Peter confesses Jesus as the Christ in Mark 8:29; but, apart from demons, the specific reference to Jesus as God's Son occurs only twice in Mark's Gospel.

[15] The Apostle's Creed was written during early church history to provide a brief summary of the Christian faith (it does not appear in the Bible, nor was it written by the apostles). Sources differ as to when the expression "descended into hell" was added since it does not appear in the earliest copies.

[16] "Hades" simply refers to the realm of departed souls, or the grave. Interestingly, the Greek version of the Apostle's Creed uses the word *hades*, not *Gehenna* (where we get the English word for hell).

[17] J. P. Lange, P. Schaff, K. Braune, and M. B. Riddle, *A Commentary on the Holy Scriptures* (Bellingham, WA: Logos Bible Software, 2008), 146. See also S. M. Baugh, *Ephesians: Evangelical Exegetical Commentary*, ed. W. H. House, H. W. Harris III, and A. W. Pitts (Bellingham, WA: Lexham Press, 2015), 327–28; E. Ritzema and J. D. Barry, "Apostles' Creed," in *The Lexham Bible Dictionary*, ed. J. D. Barry et al. (Bellingham, WA: Lexham Press, 2016); and Westminster Assembly, *The Westminster Confession of Faith: Edinburgh Edition* (Philadelphia: William S. Young, 1851), 198.

[18] In 1 Peter 4:6, the "dead" is referring to martyrs of the faith (see 1 Peter 4:19; also 2:23).

[19] Study Notes, *The ESV Study Bible* (Wheaton, IL: Crossway Bibles, 2008), 2410.

[20] While Ephesians 6:16 does refer to "fiery darts" of the devil aimed at believers, these refer to "the schemes" of the devil (referring to Satan's lies, deceptions, and temptations; see Eph. 6:11). While Satan is certainly our Adversary, his activities are described in terms of being a Tempter (Matt. 4:3), Accuser (Rev. 12:10), and Deceiver (Rev. 12:9).

[21] Inherent in preaching the gospel is the expectation to make disciples, including baptizing and teaching them (see Matt. 28:19).

[22] See Luke 10:17–19 and Acts 16:16–18, 19:11, and 28:5, 8–9.

[23] This is not to say that God no longer performs miracles today; He most certainly does! (Note: for an excellent book that addresses the specific question as to whether Christians today are instructed to cast out demons and how God's Word guides us concerning spiritual warfare, I recommend *What the Bible Teaches about Spiritual Warfare* by Robert Dean Jr. and Thomas Ice.

[24] J. C. Ryle, *Expository Thoughts on the Gospels: Luke*, vol. 1 (New York: Robert Carter and Brothers, 1897): 257.

[25] W. A. Elwell and B. J. Beitzel, "Armageddon," in *Baker Encyclopedia of the Bible*, vol. 1 (Grand Rapids, MI: Baker Book House, 1988), 171.

[26] The enemy didn't fire shots from an arrow or any other weapon.

[27] Elwell and Beitzel, "Armageddon," 171.

[28] That is, Jesus casts him into the bottomless pit, which is best understood as a temporary prison for unclean spirits; see Supplemental Reading "What Are Hades and the Abyss?" on page 194.

[29] The number may be either literal or symbolic to represent a long period of time.

[30] See Supplemental Reading, "What Are Hades and the Abyss?" on page 194.

[31] G. T. Meadors, "New Heavens and a New Earth," in *Evangelical Dictionary of Biblical Theology*, electronic ed. (Grand Rapids, MI: Baker Book House, 1996), 563.

[32] Johnston M. Cheney and Stanley A. Ellisen, *Jesus Christ: The Greatest Life—A Unique Blending of the Four Gospels* (Eugene, OR: Paradise Publishing, 1999), 110.

LEADER GUIDE

Welcome, friend!

I am so delighted you chose to lead a group through *Legion: Rediscovering the God Who Rescues Me*. May the Lord richly bless you and your group as you journey through this study!

Whether you have been leading Bible study groups for years or this is your first time, the greatest gifts we each bring to those God entrusts to our care are our support, love, and encouragement—and for these, there is no prerequisite. Nevertheless, I created a comprehensive Leader Guide to offer some helpful tips and resources to equip you as you prepare to lead your group. The fifteen-page Leader Guide for this study, as well as those for each of my other studies, is available as a free PDF download at www.shadiahrichi.com/leader-guides/.

Each Leader Guide includes the following:

- Advice before You Begin
- About the Study (also included at the start of this book)
- Practical Tips
- Group Etiquette Guidelines
- Planning and Leading Group Meetings
- Group Study Tips (also included at the start of this book)
- Suggested Schedule
- Video Sessions Guide
- Frequently Asked Questions

I am honored to partner with you and excited for all God has planned to do in you and through you!

Questions?

Please send any questions in an email to ministry@shadiahrichi.com, and either I or someone on my ministry team will get back to you right away.

TIPS FOR A SABBATH DATE WITH JESUS

THERE IS NO GREATER DIGNITY BESTOWED ON HUMAN beings than the fact that the Creator of the universe desires a relationship with us: He actually enjoys spending time with us! In fact, God is speaking to us all the time. However, we are not always listening.

More and more, our culture is conditioning us to crave noise, busyness, and entertainment—anything to distract us from nurturing our relationship with God. So before we are able to listen, we need to be able to hear, and before we can hear, we need to be silent. And before we can be silent, we need to remove ourselves from the distractions of the world.

It was quite some time before I developed the habit of setting aside time each week to spend with God (which also required adjusting some priorities); but once I did, it changed everything. Whether you already plan a weekly time with the Lord and are simply looking for some fresh ideas, or you want to begin making this a new practice, these are some tips you may find helpful.

What you'll need: Bible, pen, prayer journal, blank paper or notebook, worship music, favorite drink or snack, tissues, comfortable chair or cushion.

Where to go: a local park, library, coffee shop, your backyard, beach, state park or trails, local retreat centers (you'd be surprised how many there are!), your living room (when I stay home, I will often set up a YouTube video of a fireplace, campfire, or calm ocean waves to create atmosphere where there otherwise is none).

Planning around children's or others' schedules: If your current schedule doesn't allow you to set aside a full day, begin with a half-day or even one to two hours. If you have small children, consider arranging with your spouse or another parent to alternate spending a few hours alone with the Lord and then a few hours watching the children.

One friend who had a husband, job, and house full of children realized that the best solution for her was to leave home early on Saturday mornings and spend time with the Lord at a coffee shop. She could only go for one or two hours, but she confessed that it had become her most sacred hours of the week.

The key is to try different things until you find what works. God knows your heart, and He knows the challenges you face. Meet Him where you are, and let it grow from there.

What to do: There are numerous helpful outlines available to plan your time with the Lord; however, the key is to remember that these are merely tools. Ultimately, you want the Holy Spirit to be your guide. He may have His own agenda, such as healing an old wound, inviting you to cast your burdens on Him, or simply resting in His presence. At the same time, come prepared with your needs. He is your loving Father who cares for you. You may need to forgive someone, or perhaps God has been convicting you about something, or you might simply need His guidance. The key is to be intentional. The saying "If you aim at nothing, you are sure to hit it" holds true even in our walk with God. The simple outline that follows is one that I adapted from a class I took while at seminary. Unlike the outline that I use periodically in my morning quiet times, I prefer this outline for more strategic prayer.[1]

Prepare the night before by praying and asking God to bless the time you have committed to Him. Plan to divide your time (four hours is recommended) into quarters and dedicate each quarter to one of the following steps.

Solitude and Meditation: Take this time to clear your mind and heart and to focus on God.

- Consider starting your time by taking a walk, reading a psalm, or meditating on God's attributes.

Confession: Ask yourself what grieves God, why it grieves Him, and why it matters.

- Record in your journal what God reveals. Use your blank paper or notebook to record any action steps God lays on your heart.

Personal Prayer: Share your dreams, fears, and concerns with God.

- Open your heart and invite Him into your deepest thoughts.

Strategic Prayer: Seek God's counsel for specific questions, or ask for guidance in your areas of responsibility, such as at home, at work, or in ministry.

- Where do you need wisdom?
- Record any action steps in your notebook.

The beauty of meeting with God is that He is always willing to meet us where we are. Trust Him in this, and He will honor your commitment. "The LORD is good to those who wait for him, to the soul who seeks him. It is good that one should wait quietly for the salvation of the LORD" (Lam. 3:25–26).

Note

[1] You can download my daily Quiet Time Guide, along with a variety of other great free resources, by visiting www.shadiahrichi.com/bonus.

ALSO BY

Shadia Hrichi

ISBN 978-1-68426-301-1

If God can choose the Canaanite Tamar to continue the line through which Christ would come, can anything keep Him from weaving your story into His redemptive plan? Through this six-week in-depth Bible study, you will discover that no matter life's twists or turns or your sins and failures, there is a God redeeming everything for His glory.

"If you enjoy squeezing every delicious drop of truth from the stories found in Scripture, Shadia Hrichi's new study on Tamar will delight you. She handles God's Word with exceeding care, pointing us to the many vital lessons worth learning and applying to our own lives."

—**Liz Curtis-Higgs,** best-selling author, *Bad Girls of the Bible*

ISBN 978-0-89112-470-2

Witness the depths of God's compassion through the eyes of a runaway slave. Through this seven-week, in-depth Bible study, you will find that when you surrender your life into God's hands, your trials and triumphs serve a magnificent purpose: to draw you into the arms of the faithful *God Who Sees Me.*

"Deep and packed with surprising insights! I enjoyed exploring the story of Hagar—an often-discarded woman who played a profound part in human history. . . . This study beautifully captures the depth of God's love for all people. I am excited to share it with others!"

—**Francine Rivers,** international best-selling author

ISBN 978-1-68426-129-1

Rahab, who witnessed no miracles and knew none of God's laws, merely heard of God's power—*and believed.* Her story is centered on three key themes: *faith*, *grace*, and *salvation*. By the time you finish this six-week study, you will never look at the story of Rahab the same way again.

"Insightful and rich in cultural details, Shadia's new Bible study on Rahab takes the reader on a deep and meaningful journey. Because of it, I have a fresh understanding of the God who saves. Highly recommended."

—**Robin Lee Hatcher,** Christy Award–winning author of The Legacy of Faith series and *I'll Be Seeing You*

Visit shadiahrichi.com for updates on new books and resources in the Behind the Seen series.

LEAFWOOD PUBLISHERS
an imprint of Abilene Christian University Press